Roz Denny

modern
German
food

Over 70 contemporary recipes

SIMON & SCHUSTER

A VIACOM COMPANY

Published in Great Britain by Simon & Schuster UK Ltd
for the Central Marketing Organisation
of German Agricultural Industries
CMA House, 17a Church Road,
Wimbledon, London SW19 5DQ
First published 2001
A Viacom Company
Copyright © CMA – Central Marketing Organisation
of German Agricultural Industries
This book is copyright under the Berne Convention.
No reproduction without permission.
All rights reserved.

The right of Roz Denny to be identified as the
Author of this Work has been asserted by her in
accordance with sections 77 and 78 of the Copyright,
Designs and Patents Act, 1988.
1 3 5 7 9 10 8 6 4 2
Simon & Schuster UK Ltd
Africa House
64-78 Kingsway
London WC2B 6AH

Cover photograph: Mini Onion Tart (page 113)
Design, photography and typesetting:
Teubner Foodfoto GmbH, Füssen, Germany
China provided for photographs by
Eschenbach Hotelporzellan

Printed and bound in Italy
A CIP catalogue record for this book is available
from the British Library
ISBN 0 85941 989 4

Contents

Specialities from Germany

The chances of every man, woman and child in the UK consuming a German food and drink product each day are very high. However, it is probably true to say that few people here have a deep understanding of German cuisine. What does the 'average' German consume at home, we wonder? When travelling to or through Germany we are first and foremost struck by the very high quality of food available both in and outside homes. The reason is simple – German people love good cooking. When it comes to food, they expect the best, and they make sure they produce the best. The second impression visitors get about food in Germany is the glorious variety of regional dishes. There is an almost bewildering variety of cold meats, sausages, cheeses, beers etc. in shops, restaurants, cafés, homes and even out on the streets. This wonderful diversity is not the result of manufacturers dreaming up new products, but rather because the various regions of Germany have preserved their specialities, many of which are centuries old. It is a perfect blend of past and present.

One of the reasons for this lies in the history of the country. Until the nineteenth century Germany was a collection of individual states. Modern Germany is now a federation of 16 states (or Länder), all with their own particular styles of cooking. Although the culinary boundaries are now becoming a little blurred, there are still many dishes that one can identify as typical of a certain region.

In the north of Germany, sea fish has been cured and preserved for centuries. Cured fish travels well and so specialities such as Matjes herrings and smoked eel have become popular all over Germany. The climate and terrain in these regions are also ideal for grains such as rye and oats which are then baked into the wonderful mixed grain and seeded breads for which Germany is renowned. Orchards along the river Elbe yield apples, pears and cherries and from the lush northern pastures come a multitude of dairy goods and well-rounded cheeses. Shared borders with Baltic and Scandinavian countries have influenced the production of Schnaps, now drunk as beer chasers all over the country.

Regional names frequently preface product names. In the region of Westphalia lean, full-bodied pigs yield world-famous hams and excellent sausages eaten with rich rye breads and nutty, aromatic Pumpernickel. The name of the region Thuringia is the mark of a top-quality, tasty, meaty grilling sausage; Spreewald crisp gherkins are happily munched all over Germany and the climate and soil of Baden-Württemberg nurture the gourmet's choice of fine white asparagus, sweet juicy plums and apples from the Lake Constance region. In the south, Bavaria not only boasts the highest number of breweries in Germany, it is also the heartland of Germany's fine cheeses, wild game and forest mushrooms. It has been said that there is an imaginary border which separates the potato lovers of the north from the noodle (Spätzle) enthusiasts of the south.

The traditional farmers markets are still very much alive and kicking in every German town and city today, providing wonderful fresh regional produce. With the influence of organic farming as strong, if not stronger, in Germany than in the UK, these markets were and are the main source of organic produce and organic specialities.

One of the great joys of good cooking is working with first-class produce and serving meals you know will be received with eager anticipation. German foods more than suit the task. They have a universal appeal and suit all palates and tastes.

So enjoy… and Guten Appetit!
Roz Denny

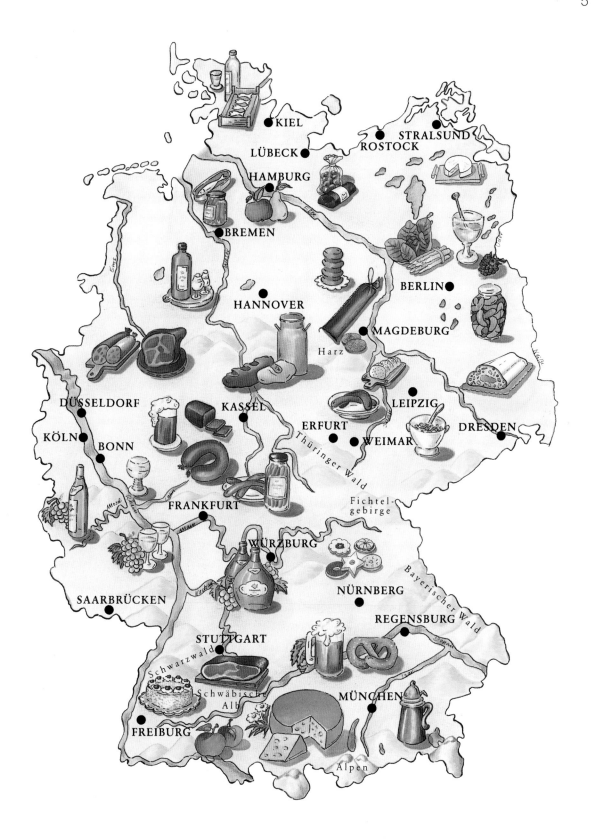

5

KIEL

STRALSUND

LÜBECK

ROSTOCK

HAMBURG

BREMEN

BERLIN

HANNOVER

MAGDEBURG

Harz

DÜSSELDORF

KASSEL

LEIPZIG

KÖLN

ERFURT

DRESDEN

BONN

WEIMAR

Thüringer Wald

FRANKFURT

Fichtel-
gebirge

WÜRZBURG

NÜRNBERG

Bayerischer Wald

SAARBRÜCKEN

REGENSBURG

STUTTGART

Schwarzwald

Schwäbische
Alb

MÜNCHEN

FREIBURG

Alpen

Soups

Soup can be an elegant, light starter to whet your appetite or it can be a substantial meal that satisfies your hunger. The Germans are great soup makers and find many opportunities to serve hot, steaming bowls of homemade recipes. Vegetables, meat broths, sliced cold meats, sausages and creamy cheese, even Sauerkraut and fruits can all form the basis of good German soup. Germans have a wonderful variety of accompaniments for soup – dumplings, pancake shreds, noodles, croûtons and toast.

Above: a consommé with broccoli garnish. The broccoli is cooked separately and added later so that the stock stays clear.

Light chicken broth

Hühnerbrühe mit Flädle

Simmer a small chicken in a pan with vegetables for a clear soup then serve the broth with vegetable and pancake shreds. The cooked chicken can be used again although you may like to use some of the breast meat, shredded finely. You can make this broth the day before, then after straining, chill and scrape off any fat that has settled on top.
Serves 4–6

1 small roasting chicken, about 1.3 kg
   (3 lb)
1 large onion
1 large leek, sliced and washed well
1 stick celery
2 carrots
2 bay leaves
fresh thyme sprig
a small glass of dry white wine (optional)
1 large pickled gherkin, cut into small thin
   sticks
sea salt and freshly ground black pepper

For the pancake batter:
50 g (1¾ oz) plain flour
1 egg
150 ml (¼ pint) milk
½ teaspoon salt
some rapeseed oil for cooking the
   pancakes

1 Pull any excess fat from inside the bird and place in a large pan. Pour over 3 litres (5¼ pints) of cold water. Bring slowly to the boil, skimming off any scum with a large metal spoon.

2 Meanwhile, prepare the vegetables. Half the quantity is simmered with the stock so only needs to be roughly chopped. Cut the remainder into thin shreds.

3 Add half the onion, the green of the leek, half the celery stick and one carrot along with the bay leaves, thyme, wine (if using) and seasoning.

Soup garnishes

Croûtons, little cubes of crisply fried bread, are always popular with soups. You can never make too many! If you do have any left over, just store them in an airtight container. German cooks use not only white bread, but also light rye bread. You'll also find that Pumpernickel makes good croûtons too.

Cut medium thick slices of bread from a whole loaf. Remove the crusts and cut the bread into 1 cm (½-inch) cubes. Fry in shallow rapeseed oil heated to a medium high temperature, turning the cubes in the oil until golden and crispy. Drain on paper towels.

You can vary your croûtons by adding different flavours. For herb cubes simply sprinkle the cubes with dried mixed herbs in the pan as they fry. For garlic cubes, heat 2 fat garlic cloves in the pan with about 6 tablespoons of rapeseed oil over a low heat so the flavour is absorbed. Remove the garlic then toss in the bread cubes. For curry-flavoured cubes, sprinkle in pinches of mild curry powder as the cubes cook.

4 Return to a simmer and cook uncovered for about an hour, by which time the chicken will be nicely cooked and the liquid reduced by about half.

5 Meanwhile, thinly slice or shred the rest of the vegetables to serve with the broth along with the gherkins.

6 Make the pancakes now. Whizz the flour, egg, milk and salt to a smooth batter in a food processor or blender.

7 Heat a little oil in a small frying pan or pancake pan. When you can feel a good heat rising, pour in about 2 tablespoons of the batter and swirl round the pan so it fills the base.

8 Cook until the liquid disappears and little holes appear. Loosen the edges and flip the pancake over to cook the other side for a few seconds.

9 Shake out of the pan on to a plate and cover with a clean tea towel. Repeat with the remaining batter until you have a stack of at least 4 pancakes. You may get more – lucky you! Roll the pancakes up one at a time and cut into thin shreds. Cover and set aside.

10 Strain the soup through a large muslin-lined colander (or use a clean household cloth, e.g. a J-cloth). Discard the chopped vegetables but save the chicken for another use, unless you want to shred some of the chicken breast to serve.

11 Measure and return the stock to the pan; boil to reduce to about 1.5 litres (2¾ pints) if necessary. Now add the shredded fresh vegetables and simmer for 10 minutes. Add the gherkin sticks, check the seasoning and serve piping hot.

Farmer's market in
Bavaria

Sauerkraut soup
Sauerkrautsuppe

Sauerkraut lends itself nicely to a winter warming soup. This is more of a main meal soup to which you can add slices of your favourite smoked German sausage. Chunks of rye bread are a good accompaniment.
Serves 4

500 g jar Sauerkraut
250 g (9 oz) Katenspeck, in a piece
1 onion, chopped
1 fat garlic clove, crushed
1 litre (1¾ pints) cold water
½ teaspoon ground paprika
2 teaspoons chopped fresh dill
about 125 g (4½ oz) smoked German
    sausage of your choice, sliced or
    chopped
142 ml carton soured cream
sea salt and freshly ground black pepper

1 Rinse the Sauerkraut in cold water and leave to drain.

2 De-rind the Katenspeck, cut out any little bones and chop small.

3 Place the Sauerkraut, onion, garlic and cold water in a large saucepan with seasoning.

Bring to the boil, then simmer for 15 minutes.

4 Meanwhile, fry the chopped Katenspeck in a dry frying pan until the fat starts to run. Stir in the paprika and mix into the Sauerkraut mixture. Return to a gentle simmer for another 15 minutes then add the dill and sausage of your choice. Stir in the cream, check the seasoning and reheat until just on the point of boiling. Serve.

Split pea and sausage soup
Erbsensuppe mit Würstchen

A truly nourishing soup – high in protein, fibre and flavour. It is also very versatile because not only can you serve it as a starter, it can double as a wholesome light meal with a chunk of crusty rye bread. Make it with green split peas and chopped fried Katenspeck. The stock for this recipe could be chicken or beef made with German organic stock cubes, or use the cooking liquid from boiling a ham. It is quite thick, so if you prefer it thinner, simply add extra water.
Serves 4–6

250 g (9 oz) dried green split peas, soaked
    overnight
50 g (1¾ oz) Katenspeck
1 onion, chopped
1 potato, chopped
1.5 litres (2¾ pints) chicken, beef or ham
    stock – fresh or from a cube
½ teaspoon dried marjoram or oregano,
    or a good pinch of dried thyme
1 pair of small, whole Frankfurters
sea salt and freshly ground black pepper
a little chopped fresh parsley or chervil, to
    serve

1 Drain the soaked peas and rinse in cold water. Set aside. Sauté the Speck or bacon in a large saucepan for a few minutes over a medium heat until the fat starts to run, then stir in the onion and potato. Continue to sauté for 5 minutes until softened.

2 Add the peas, stock, herbs and pepper to taste. Bring to the boil, stirring once or twice, and allow to boil for 5 minutes. Then partially cover the pan and turn the heat down to a gentle simmer, stirring occasionally.

3 Cook for 30–40 minutes until thickened and the peas are soft. If you like, you can blend the soup in a food processor or blender, but it looks more wholesome with a rustic chunkiness. Heat the Frankfurters in a little hot water. Check the seasoning, adding salt if required. If you have used ham stock you may not need it. Sprinkle with a little chopped fresh parsley or chervil if liked, and garnish with the Frankfurters.

The Frankfurter

From humble origins in Frankfurt's 'sausage quarter' the Frankfurter has crossed class and national boundaries to bring a taste of its home town to afficionados worldwide. Present at coronations of emperors, Frankfurters were known as 'coronation sausages'. They are also called Vienna sausages, because they were popularised there by an expatriate German butcher early in the 19th century. Imitations soon abounded, until in 1929 the name was restricted to sausages made only with pork and spices and no additives, ensuring that today afficionados can be guaranteed the smoky delicacy of the genuine article.

Courgette soup with Pumpernickel and Quark toasts

Zucchinisuppe und Pumpernickeltoast mit Kräuterquark

Pumpernickel makes delicious little toasted croûtes which can be spread with green-herb-flavoured Quark to float on top of soup or served alongside. A light creamed vegetable soup such as courgette, carrot, kohlrabi or mushroom would be a good base to serve them with. The spinach leaves give this soup a fresh green colour.

Serves 4–6

50 g (1¾ oz) butter
1 onion, chopped
1 garlic clove, crushed
3 large courgettes, trimmed and chopped
a good handful of fresh spinach leaves,
**   roughly chopped (optional)**
1.2 litres (2 pints) chicken or vegetable
**   stock, preferably fresh**
150 g (5½ oz) Quark
3 slices Pumpernickel
a little fresh lemon juice
2-3 tablespoons chopped mixed fresh
**   herbs e.g. parsley, chives, basil, dill or**
**   marjoram**
sea salt and freshly ground black pepper

1 Melt the butter in a large saucepan and sauté the onion, garlic and courgette gently for about 10 minutes, stirring once or twice. Do not let them brown.

2 Add the spinach and cook until wilted then pour in the stock. Bring to the boil, season to taste then stir in and simmer, partially covered, for about 10–15 minutes.

3 Strain the vegetables and reserve the liquid. Pass the vegetables through a food processor or blender, gradually adding back the liquid and adding 2 tablespoons of the Quark. Return the soup to the pan and set aside.

4 Either cut the Pumpernickel into small rounds using a scone cutter or leave whole. Toast under a hot grill for 1–2 minutes until just crisp. Remove, cut into quarters if not already cut into rounds, and allow to cool.

5 Beat the herbs and some seasoning into the rest of the Quark. When ready to serve, spread the Quark on the Pumpernickel toasts. Bring the soup to the boil and check the seasoning, adding a little lemon juice if you think it needs it. Divide the soup between warmed bowls and top or serve with the Pumpernickel toasts.

Dumplings

Up until about two hundred years ago only the wealthy ate potatoes, and the bread dumpling was the staple fare of the Bavarian masses. The legend of the inhabitants of Munich using dumplings to defend themselves against the Bohemian King Ottokar in ancient times is repeated maliciously on occasions, but many more peaceful and delicious variations are enjoyed today using cheese, pork, milk, or even potato! On Sundays the humble everyday breadcrumb recipe is traditionally enlivened with liver.

Beetroot and kohlrabi soup with rye bread dumplings

Rote Bete-Kohlrabi-Suppe mit Klößchen

Kohlrabi is a root vegetable much enjoyed by Germans, and becoming more easily available in the UK. It looks a little unusual with stalks sticking directly out of the flesh but many top chefs rate its fine flavour. Beetroot has a delicious sweet, aromatic flavour so it seems a good idea to marry them together in a soup. Add small light dumplings made with rye breadcrumbs. In Germany, finely chopped beef marrow is used to enrich dumplings – you might find shredded beef suet a reasonable substitute. Vegetarians could use vegetable suet or a little melted butter. Wear rubber gloves when peeling the beetroot to stop the flesh staining your fingers! Serves 4–6

2 tablespoons rapeseed oil
25 g (1 oz) butter
500 g (1 lb 2 oz) raw beetroot, peeled thinly and chopped
1 kohlrabi, peeled thinly and chopped
1 onion, chopped
2 sticks celery, chopped + leaves to garnish
a good pinch of cumin or caraway seeds
1 teaspoon ground coriander
a small glass of red wine
1.5 litres (2¾ pints) vegetable or chicken stock or water
sea salt and freshly ground black pepper
For the dumplings:
80 g (3 oz) wholemeal rye breadcrumbs
80 g (3 oz) self-raising flour
2 tablespoons shredded suet or 40 g (1½ oz) melted and cooled butter
3 tablespoons chopped fresh parsley (optional)
1 medium egg, beaten

1 Heat the oil and butter in a large saucepan and stir in the beetroot, kohlrabi, onion and celery. Cover and sweat all the vegetables on a low heat for about 10 minutes shaking the pan once or twice, but do not lift the lid.

2 Add the cumin or caraway and the coriander, then cook for another minute. Stir in the wine, cook for 2 more minutes, then pour in the stock or water. Season to taste then bring to the boil. Simmer, partially covered, for 20 minutes until the vegetables are very tender.

3 Meanwhile, make the dumplings. Mix the breadcrumbs, flour, suet or butter (beef marrow if possible) with a little seasoning and the parsley. Mix to a firm dough with the beaten egg, adding it gradually as you may not need it all. Shape into 8 dumplings, using wet fingers if necessary. Keep to one side.

4 Strain the vegetables, reserving the liquid. Pass the vegetables through a food processor or blender, gradually adding the liquid until you have a smooth, light soup.

5 Return the soup to a gentle boil and drop in the dumplings. Cover and simmer for 10 minutes. Do not allow the liquid to bubble too hard or it will break up the dumplings.

6 Serve in warmed bowls garnished with the celery leaves. It will look very pretty.

Pumpkin and salami soup

Kürbissuppe mit Salami

Don't keep salami just for salads and snacks. Try adding it to hot dishes like pork or beef stews, pop on top of pizzas or scatter over soups. In this recipe, the full smoky flavour is nicely balanced by the creamy sweetness of pumpkin. There are many great German salamis to choose from – such as Sommerwurst, Cervelat and the various coated salamis – herb, onion and more recently apple chunks. Serves 4–6

2 tablespoons rapeseed oil
25 g (1 oz) butter
500 g (1 lb 2 oz) fresh pumpkin flesh, diced
1 onion, chopped
1 large garlic clove, crushed
½ teaspoon mild curry powder
a good pinch of dried thyme
1.2 litres (2 pints) chicken or vegetable stock (can be made with a cube)
2–3 tablespoons cream
100 g (3½ oz) German salami, any variety, cut into shreds or quarters

sea salt and freshly ground black pepper
flat leaf parsley leaves or chervil sprigs, to garnish

1 Heat the oil and butter in a large saucepan and gently sauté the pumpkin with the onion and garlic for about 5 minutes until softened.

2 Add the curry and thyme and cook for one minute then stir in the stock. Bring to the boil, season and simmer, partially covered, for about 15–20 minutes until the flesh is very soft.

3 Strain off the liquid and reserve. Pass the solids through a food processor or blender and whizz until smooth, adding the reserved liquid.

4 Return to the pan and bring back to the boil. Stir in the cream and then check the seasoning. Pour into warmed soup plates and gently stir through the salami pieces. Sprinkle with the parsley leaves or chervil sprigs and serve with chunks of rye bread.

Chilled plum soup

Zwetschen-kaltschale

German people love fruit soups served lightly chilled during their fine, hot summers.

The plums they use are from the Baden region which have the right balance of sweetness and piquant sourness. The soup itself couldn't be easier to make. Serve smooth and chilled in pretty dessert bowls topped with a little Quark sweetened and flavoured with vanilla and lemon. An unusual and delicious dessert or light first course.

Serves 4

600 g (1 lb 4 oz) ripe German plums
1 litre (1¾ pints) water
1–2 tablespoons caster sugar, depending
**   on sweetness of plums + extra for**
**   Quark**
1 large cinnamon stick
4 whole cloves
grated zest and juice of 1 small lemon
100 g (3½ oz) tub Quark
2 tablespoons milk
a few drops of vanilla essence
a little ground cinnamon, to dust, optional

1 Halve the plums and remove the stones. Place the fruit in a saucepan with the water, sugar to taste and the whole spices.

2 Bring to a boil, then partially cover and simmer very gently for about 20 minutes until the fruit is very soft. Remove the whole spices then rub the fruit though a sieve with the back of a ladle or pass through a food processor or blender. Mix together with the liquor, stir in the lemon juice and check the sweetness. Don't make it too sweet though, it should be light and refreshing. Cool and chill.

3 When ready to serve, beat the Quark with the milk and some sugar to taste adding the lemon zest and vanilla. Pour the soup into chilled bowls (ideally pretty glass ones). Spoon dollops of Quark into the centre of the soup. Dust with some ground cinnamon for decoration. Serve with crisp German biscuits. Perfect!

Mushroom and Bavarian blue brie cappuccino soup

Pilzschaumsüppchen mit Blauschimmelbrie

Make a light and smooth mushroom soup then stir in some creamy Bavarian blue brie cheese and froth with an electric blender for the ultimate in delicious chic. Serve in small tea or coffee cups.

Serves 6

2 large shallots, chopped
1 garlic clove, crushed
2 tablespoons rapeseed oil
15 g (½ oz) dried ceps (optional)
25 g (1 oz) butter
250 g (9 oz) brown button mushrooms,
**   finely chopped**
a small glass of dry white wine
2 tablespoons flour
1 litre (1¾ pints) chicken or vegetable
**   stock**
a good pinch of dried thyme
4 tablespoons double cream
100 g (3½ oz) Bavarian blue brie
sea salt and freshly ground black pepper

**2 teaspoons very finely chopped parsley
    to garnish (optional)**

1 In a large pan, sauté the shallots and garlic in 1 tablespoon of the oil for 5 minutes until softened. Meanwhile, soak the ceps, if used, in boiling water to cover until cool.

2 Add the remaining oil and butter to the pan, heat until melted, then stir in the chopped mushrooms to coat in the oil. Cover and sweat for 10 minutes until softened, shaking the pan occasionally.

3 Pour in the wine and cook until evaporated. Stir in the flour and cook for a minute or two.

4 Add the stock and the water that the ceps were soaked in, if used. Add the thyme and seasoning. Chop the soaked ceps finely, if used, and add to the pan. Bring to the boil stirring, then simmer for 15 minutes, partially covered.

5 Strain out the mushrooms reserving the liquid. Whizz mushrooms in a food processor until very smooth, scraping down the sides once or twice and adding the reserved liquid back slowly. You do need to keep the machine whizzing for longer than normal for a wonderfully smooth texture.

6 Pass the soup back into the saucepan through a sieve and rub the purée with the back of a ladle. Discard any solids that will not pass through. Stir in the cream and return to a gentle boil.

7 Meanwhile, cut the rinds from the cheese and divide into small chunks. On the lowest heat possible, mix in the cheese, stirring until smooth. Check the seasoning. Do not allow it to boil again.

8 Take a hand blender and whizz the soup until a good head of foam appears.

9 Pour the soup into warmed cups, holding back the foam with a palette knife or large metal spoon. When most of the soup has been poured in the cups, give the remaining liquid one final whizz and spoon the foam into the cups. Sprinkle the tops with little pinches of chopped parsley or grind over some black pepper. Serve immediately.

**The most important
and versatile meat in the
German kitchen, ideal for meals
at all times of the day**

Sausages

REGENSBURGER Half pork
and half beef, double smoked
before and after cooking. Serve
hot or cold.

A butcher removing German meat sausage
(Fleischwurst) and Regensburger sausage
from the smoker.

Only top-grade meat is used for German sausages
and great attention is paid to consistency of quality.
Variations in sausage styles are due to blends of
meat (pork, beef, veal or poultry), the size of
mincing (fine or coarse), spices and herbs and
smoking, where relevant. Individual smoke flavours
come from natural woods, not artificial flavourings.
German sausages are recognised throughout the
world and many cooks find that if they always have
a selection of three or four in the fridge at all times,
they are never short of a good meal idea.

19

TRUFFLE LIVER PATÉ (Trüffelleberwurst) Gourmet paté spiked with aromatic black truffles. Spread on to hot toast or crostini.

SNACK SALAMI (Minisalami) Finely minced beef, pork and bacon, seasoned with spices and smoked. Ideal for lunchboxes.

PEPPER COATED SALAMI (Salami im Pfeffermantel) Add a little extra spice to your cold meat platter with pepper coated salami.

CERVELAT (Cervelatwurst) Milder than salami and containing no garlic. Made from finely minced pork and beef. Mildly smoked.

GREEN PEPPER COATED SALAMI (Salami mit grünem Pfeffer) Coated in attractive light green peppercorns.

SUMMER SAUSAGE (Sommerwurst) A mildly seasoned salami speciality, dried and matured and smoked over beechwood.

GERMAN MEAT SAUSAGE (Fleischwurst) A mildly smoked sausage. Serve sliced or added to pasta, soups and salads.

HAM SAUSAGE (Bierschinken) With extra pieces of ham, lightly spiced and then smoked over beech, ash and juniper wood.

POULTRY SAUSAGE (Geflügelwurst) Poultry sausage is ideal for people watching their weight. Low in fat and high in protein.

HOT SMOKED SALAMI (Kochsalami) A traditional cooked and hot-smoked Bavarian salami. Slice very thinly.

NUREMBERG GRILLING SAUSAGE (Nürnberger Würstchen) Germany's most famous mini grilling sausage.

BEER SAUSAGE (Bierwurst) Served in Germany with a cold glass of beer. Flavoured with a little garlic and spices.

BOCKWURST Made from finely minced and spiced pork and beef then smoked.

BRATWURST The ultimate German street and barbecue food. Thick and juicy grilling sausages served in warm crusty rolls.

FRANKFURTER Possibly the world's most famous sausage! Made from finely minced pork then cold smoked.

Salads

Salads are a common feature on many German dining tables, either as side dishes, as starters or as quick, light meals. Many of the ingredients can be bought ready prepared – these include sliced cold meats, cheeses, pickled fish and vegetables. Close to the heart of most Germans is potato salad, for many the ultimate comfort food. Nearly everyone has their own favourite recipe – these might feature diced new potatoes, or chopped old potatoes or even fork-crushed floury potatoes tossed with hot meat stock and dressing.

Above: a salad of asparagus, radishes, rocket, peppers, cheese, lettuce, Black Forest ham and radicchio with a vinaigrette containing some chopped hard-boiled egg.

Basic oil and vinegar dressing

Grundrezept Salatsauce

Wine and apple vinegars are the most popular vinegars used in German salad dressings. Apple vinegar gives a light fruity flavour. To keep the dressing light use the neutral flavoured rapeseed oil. For added flavour, German mustards provide variety, from sweet and mild to hot and with herbs. This dressing is a good all-purpose recipe for green leaf, potato, pasta and mixed vegetable salads. Make a batch and store in a screw–topped jar in the fridge. Shake well to blend each time. Makes 300 ml (½ pint)

**200 ml (7 fl oz) rapeseed oil (or 100 ml/
    3½ fl oz each rapeseed and olive oil)**
**100 ml (3½ fl oz) white wine or German
    apple vinegar, or half of each**
½ teaspoon sea salt
**1 teaspoon German mustard, sweet or
    medium hot**
**1 teaspoon German flower honey
    (optional)**
¼ teaspoon freshly ground black pepper

Whisk all the ingredients together in a jug then pour into a screw-topped jar. Alternatively, measure the ingredients directly into a jar, seal and shake well to blend. However, be sure you have mixed in all the ingredients well. A whisk is a surer bet. It will store for a good month in the fridge.

Variations
You can vary the flavour of this basic dressing with any of the following additions:
• **chopped fresh parsley, dill, basil, chervil
    or marjoram**
• **a teaspoon of horseradish relish**
• **a teaspoon or two of finely chopped
    gherkins**
• **2–3 rashers of Katenspeck, grilled until
    crisp then crushed**

Creamy Quark dressing

Cremiges Quark-Dressing

This is a very versatile, low-fat, creamy dressing, delicious with crisp green salad leaves or baby new potatoes, shredded chicken, shredded cheese, diced ham and frankfurters. Makes 300 ml (10 fl oz)

1 teaspoon sea salt
¼ teaspoon freshly ground black pepper
½ teaspoon caster sugar
1 teaspoon coarse-grain German mustard
1 garlic clove, crushed
2 tablespoons rapeseed oil
250 g tub Quark
**1–2 tablespoons chopped fresh parsley
    (optional)**

1 Beat the salt, pepper, sugar, mustard, garlic and oil in a bowl with a small whisk.

2 Gradually whisk in the Quark until smooth and creamy. Stir in the parsley, if used. It will keep for about 3 days stored in the fridge. To thin this dressing to a coating consistency, simply mix in 3–4 tablespoons of milk.

Chives at a market

Summer herb dip
Sommerlicher Kräuter-Dip

In the heat of the summer our taste buds long for cool, crisp vegetables and light creamy dressings and dips – so refreshing and easy to eat. Quark makes a quick light dip that can be blended together in a few minutes. Even better it has far fewer calories than richer cream cheese or mayonnaise dips. So you can have a bigger portion!

Serves 4–6

250 g tub Quark
142 ml carton single cream, or 140 g
    carton low-fat natural yogurt
1 garlic clove, crushed
2 salad onions, chopped finely
3 tablespoons chopped fresh parsley
2 tablespoons chopped fresh dill
2 tablespoons chopped fresh mint or
    coriander
a couple of good pinches ground cumin
1 tablespoon fresh lemon juice
sea salt and freshly ground black pepper

For the crudités:
½ cucumber
3 medium carrots
1 white radish
a bunch fresh radishes
1 red, 1 yellow and 1 green pepper
2–3 sticks young celery stalks

1 Simply mix the Quark with the cream or yogurt in a mixing bowl. Add the garlic, onion, herbs, cumin, lemon and plenty of seasoning. Spoon into an attractive small bowl and keep chilled until nearly ready to serve.

2 Prepare the crudités. Cut the cucumber into short lengths and remove the seeds. Chop into finger-size lengths.

3 Peel the carrots and white radish. Cut into pieces the same size as the cucumber. Trim the red radishes of roots and most of the leaves. Leave at least one leaf for garnish.

4 Halve, core and slice the peppers into sticks. Slice the celery into sticks. Serve with the Quark dip.

Sunflower

Red cabbage salad with smoked cheese

Rotkohlsalat mit Räucherkäse

A colourful salad for the buffet table to be served as a side salad for sliced cold meats or as a vegetarian main meal.
Serves 4–6

1 x 500 g jar German pickled red cabbage, drained well
½ small onion, sliced thinly
½ small green pepper, cored and sliced thinly
1 teaspoon poppy seeds
2 tablespoons rapeseed oil
150 g (5 oz) Bavarian smoked cheese
sea salt and freshly ground black pepper
large leaves of light green lettuce, to serve
croûtons (optional)

1 Put the cabbage into a large bowl and toss in the sliced onion, green pepper and poppy seeds. Season to taste then mix in the oil.

2 Cut the cheese into small cubes and mix lightly into the bowl.

3 Line a platter with salad leaves and pile on the cabbage salad. A handful of ready-made croûtons would add interest and a nice crunch.

Celeriac and ham salad with mustard mayonnaise

Sellerie-Schinken-Salat mit Senfmajonäse

Celeriac is a very versatile vegetable, which in Britain we are gradually beginning to appreciate. German cooks use it in salads and as an accompaniment when hot. It looks like a knobbly turnip, has a delicate celery flavour, and is increasingly easy to buy in supermarkets. It is particularly good served with a creamy mustard dressing mixed in with the strips of lean smoked Brunswick ham.
Serves 4

some fresh lemon juice
1 celeriac
100 g (3½ oz) fine green beans, trimmed and halved
3 tablespoons Basic Oil and Vinegar Dressing (page 22)
100 g (3½ oz) Westphalian or Brunswick ham, cut into strips
100 g (3½ oz) smoked German cheese, cut into cubes
1 pickled mustard cucumber, drained well and chopped
sea salt and freshly ground black pepper

For the dressing:
2 tablespoons mayonnaise
1 tablespoon sweet German mustard
2 tablespoons Quark

1 Have ready a large bowl of cold water with some fresh lemon juice squeezed in. Cut the celeriac in quarters. Peel and cut into thin matchstick lengths, dropping them into the water as you go.

2 Bring a pan of salted water to the boil. Drain the celeriac then boil for 2 minutes. Add the green beans to the pan and continue boiling for 2 more minutes. Drain in a colander and run cold water over the vegetables to cool.

3 Place in a mixing bowl, season and toss with the Basic Oil and Vinegar Dressing. Leave to stand for 15 minutes or so while you prepare the rest of the salad.

4 Beat the dressing ingredients together and mix into the celeriac bowl. Gently stir through the ham, cheese and chopped mustard cucumber. Check the seasoning and serve. Alternatively, make the day before, cover and chill.

White asparagus with Black Forest ham

Weisser Spargel mit Schwarzwälder Schinken

A real easy-eating treat – blanched white asparagus with fine air-dried ham and a popular bistro salad.
Serves 4

500 g (1 lb 2 oz) fresh white asparagus
1 large ripe avocado
100 ml (3½ fl oz) Basic Oil and Vinegar Dressing (page 22)
4 ripe round or plum tomatoes, skinned
4 large fresh basil leaves, torn into shreds
8 wafer-thin slices Black Forest ham
1 tablespoon chopped fresh chives
sea salt and freshly ground black pepper

1 Trim the bases of the asparagus and peel with a swivel vegetable peeler. Bring a large pan of salted water to the boil and drop in the spears. Simmer for 3 minutes only. Have a large bowl of iced water at the ready.

2 Using a large slotted spoon, lift out the asparagus spears carefully. Place immediately into the iced water and leave for 5 minutes, then carefully drain in a colander.

3 Slice the avocado and mix gently with a third of the dressing. Season well. Slice the tomatoes thinly and season. Allow to stand for 10 minutes then drizzle with another third of the dressing and mix in the basil.

4 Arrange 2 slices of ham on four large plates. Divide the asparagus, tomato and avocado between the plates. Drizzle the last of the dressing over the asparagus and scatter with the chives. Season with coarsely ground black pepper and serve.

Pepper brie and radicchio salad
Brie mit grünen Pfefferkörnern auf Radicchiosalat

German brie cheese spiked with green peppercorns makes a nice basis for a main meal salad. Serve on a radicchio salad.
Serves 4

1 head radicchio
¼ head iceberg lettuce
2 tomatoes, quartered, de-seeded and
    sliced
2 spring onions, sliced into thin lengths
2 tablespoons sunflower seeds (optional)
200 g (7 oz) Bavarian brie with
    peppercorns
sea salt and freshly ground black pepper
For the dressing:
5 tablespoons rapeseed oil
2 tablespoons white wine or apple vinegar
4 teaspoons coarse-grain German
    mustard
1 teaspoon German flower honey
sea salt and freshly ground black pepper

1   First, whisk the dressing ingredients together with some salt and pepper and set aside.

2 Cut the core from the radicchio then separate the leaves. Wash and dry carefully. Tear into bite-size pieces and place in a large bowl. Prepare the iceberg lettuce in the same way. Mix with the tomato slices, most of the spring onions (reserving some for garnish) and sunflower seeds, if used.

3 Toss with half the dressing, add more seasoning if liked, then divide between four plates.

4 Cut the rind from the cheese then slice into eight. Place two on each plate, drizzle over the last of the dressing and scatter over the remaining spring onion shreds.

A venerable beech tree in Bavaria

German-style chef's salad
Chef-Salat nach deutscher Art

A large plate or bowl of a main meal salad with a base of crisp salad leaves and a fine selection of German cold meats, hams and cheeses makes an ideal light main meal for a summer or week-end lunch. Serve with sliced rye breads and a glass or two of German beer. There are many German meats you could choose from – as a guide make sure you include at least three contrasting in colour and texture including some sliced Bierwurst, a coated salami and maybe some ham sausage. For cheeses choose from Emmenthal, Tilsiter or organic mountain cheese.
Serves 4

1 small iceberg, Webb's or Cos lettuce
100 g bag wild rocket
1 small fennel bulb
125 g (4½ oz) broad beans, cooked and
   drained
2 salad onions, chopped
1 small red pepper, cored and sliced thinly
200 g (7 oz) selection sliced German cold
   meats e.g. salamis, Bierwurst, ham
   sausage, Sommerwurst
100 g (3½ oz) Frankfurters or Bockwurst
150 g (5½ oz) German cheese, sliced – e.g.
   Emmenthal, Tilsiter, etc.
150 ml (¼ pint) Basic Oil and Vinegar
   Dressing (page 22)
2 tablespoons Quark
about 8 cherry tomatoes, halved
2–3 gherkins, chopped
sea salt and freshly ground black pepper

1 Tear the lettuce into bite-sized pieces. Wash and dry carefully. Wash and dry the rocket too if necessary. Put both in a large bowl.

2 Trim the top of the fennel bulb, saving any leafy fronds, which can be used as garnish. Halve the fennel and cut out the base core, then slice the flesh very thinly. Mix into the bowl with the broad beans, onions and pepper. Season and toss all together.

3 Slice your choice of meats into shreds and cut the Frankfurters or Bockwurst into rounds. Slice the cheese into shreds.

4 Beat the dressing with the Quark. When ready to serve, mix the dressing into the bowl with the mixed salad, tossing everything well. Divide between four plates or wide bowls.

5 Arrange the meats, cheese and tomatoes on top. Scatter with the fennel leaves and chopped gherkins, grind over black pepper and serve.

Allotments

In Germany these urban oases or Schrebergärten are named after Dr. Schreber, the pioneer of communal healthy living and an inspiration to self-sufficiency enthusiasts throughout Germany. Dr. Schreber had a vision of a paradise of productivity where each member of the family could do their bit. The aim of these communes would be to provide healthy exercise for the outer person and fresh food for the inner person. But the dream wasn't realised until the good doctor had been well dug in himself; in 1870 two years after his death, his friend and co-worker Karl Gesell established the first fully-functioning model in Leipzig.

Odette's potato salad

Odette's Kartoffelsalat

Odette is a busy working mother living in Bavaria. This is her all time favourite potato salad. It uses firm salad potatoes that have been steeped in hot broth just after cooking. Make it a few hours before you intend serving it, so the flavours mellow.
Serves 4–6

500 g (1 lb 2 oz) salad potatoes, scrubbed
300 ml (½ pint) hot chicken or beef stock
5–6 tablespoons rapeseed oil
2 tablespoons white wine vinegar or apple
    vinegar
1 teaspoon German mustard
½ teaspoon caster sugar
½ teaspoon sea salt
⅓ cucumber
1 large pickled gherkin
150 g (5 oz) Katenspeck, de-rinded and
    chopped (optional)
2 shallots, chopped finely
2 salad onions, chopped finely

2 tablespoons chopped fresh chives
about 6–8 cherry tomatoes, halved
freshly ground black pepper

1 Cut the potatoes into large dice and boil in salted water until tender. Drain and pour the hot stock over them. Leave until cool, by which time they should have absorbed the stock.

2 Whisk the oil with the vinegar, mustard, sugar, salt and pepper.

3 Halve the cucumber lengthways, scoop out the seeds with a teaspoon and chop the flesh into dice. Chop the gherkin to the same size.

4 Now mix the Katenspeck, cucumber, gherkin, shallots, salad onion, chives and dressing into the cooled potatoes. Gently mix in the tomatoes and set aside in the fridge for an hour or two. Check the seasoning and serve.

New potato and Bierwurst salad with mustard cream dressing

Salat von neuen Kartoffeln mit cremigem Senfdressing

This is a good salad to serve at a barbecue or party buffet. Use baby new potatoes.
Serves 6

600 g (1 lb 5 oz) baby new potatoes, scrubbed and cut in half
½ small red onion, sliced thinly
2 tablespoons Basic Oil and Vinegar Dressing (page 22)
1 dessert apple, e.g. Jonagold
a little fresh lemon juice
100 g (3½ oz) German Bierwurst sausage, sliced thinly
2 gherkins, chopped
3 tablespoons mayonnaise
1 tablespoon German mustard
2 tablespoons Quark
1-2 tablespoons milk
a little chopped dill and fresh parsley
sea salt and freshly ground black pepper

1 Boil the potatoes in salted water for 10–12 minutes until just tender. Drain and toss into a large bowl with the sliced red onion. Season and cool.

2 Toss with the dressing and allow to get quite cold. Meanwhile, chop the apple and mix with a little lemon juice. Mix into the potato along with the Bierwurst and gherkins.

3 Beat the mayonnaise, mustard, Quark and just enough milk to make a dressing the consistency of single cream. Stir this carefully into the salad, spoon into a serving dish and sprinkle with the chopped herbs. Serve at room temperature.

Potato salads

It's amazing how versatile one vegetable can become. You can make salads with floury and waxy potatoes, old and baby new varieties. There's a German variety to suit all styles. German potato salads are not just for serving at the cold table. There are many hot dishes that are complemented by a good potato salad. The most simple and sublime are freshly grilled meaty Bratwursts, complete with a nice dollop of German mustard. Finally, a simple serving tip – don't serve potato salad straight from the fridge. It is best only lightly chilled so remove it a good half an hour before serving.

BLACK FOREST HAM (Schwarzwälder Schinken) A top quality smoked and cured ham sold in wafer thin slices with a layer of delicious creamy fat on top. Don't pull this off – it is part of the taste experience. Made from a single boneless joint with a pronounced smoky flavour. Ideal for starters.

KATENSPECK RASHERS These slices of Katenspeck can either be eaten cold or grilled lightly for German-style eggs and bacon.

Germany's top hams are known the world over as the ultimate in sliced cured pork products

Ham

All hams are first cured then either air-dried or cooked and often smoked. Great attention is paid to selecting top breeds of pigs that provide fine flavoured lean and succulent meat. Brines and smoking bring individuality to each style adding to the variety. There's a German ham to suit every meal occasion from family suppers to special entertaining.

AIR-DRIED SMOKED HAM Cured with only sea salt and matured for 10–12 months. This lean, air-dried ham is sold in wafer thin slices. Exceptionally mild.

KATENSPECK Katen is the German word for 'barn', meaning that this ham is made farmhouse style. It is cured, smoked and cooked.

WESTPHALIAN SMOKED HAM (Westfälischer Schinken) A gently flavoured ham smoked over juniper wood and left to mature for several weeks.

DARK SMOKED COOKED HAM (Kochschinken) Highest quality premium ham off the bone, smoked over beechwood chips.

LIGHT SMOKED HAM (Kochschinken) A real traditional German cooked ham. Smoked over beechwood and very mild.

COOKED HAM (Kochschinken) German hams are of high quality and contain no water. Flavour varies according to the type of cure.

LEBERKÄSE A very popular high quality meatloaf made from minced pork and beef. Leberkäse can be eaten hot or cold.

KASSELER (smoked pork loin) The ultimate ultra-lean pork loin joint, Kasseler is first cured in brine and then smoked over juniper berries. It has a fairly mild flavour.

Fish

Although Germany only has a northern coast, people in all regions are great fish eaters. Most towns and markets have fishmongers. Fresh sea fish and seafood is sold alongside many types of pickled, smoked and cured fish. There is a great tradition of eating river and lake fish, such as pike, perch, carp, trout and crayfish. Fish might be teamed with smoky Katenspeck, mustards and even Sauerkraut, so it is not surprising it is so popular.

Above: a fillet of cod with straw potato chips, peas and asparagus tips.

Pretzel seller selling
freshly baked pretzels
and pretzel rolls

Crispy fish in pretzel crumbs

Fisch in knuspriger Hülle

This should prove very popular with children, it's almost like homemade fish fingers, except much healthier and more tasty. Use any white fish fillets and crush the pretzels to crumbs in a plastic bag or food processor.
Serves 4

1 x 75 g pack pretzel sticks
about 400 g (14 oz) white fish fillets, skinned
1 large free-range egg, beaten
some rapeseed oil for frying
a selection of salad leaves, to serve
sea salt and freshly ground black pepper
For the sauce:
1 small onion, chopped
1 fat garlic clove, crushed
1 tablespoon rapeseed oil
a good knob of butter
1 x 400 g can chopped tomatoes
½ teaspoon dried basil or oregano
a good pinch of sugar
3 tablespoons Quark

1 Crush the pretzels to fine crumbs, either in a thick plastic bag with a rolling pin or in a food processor.

2 Check the fish for fine bones with your fingertips and pull out any you can feel. Cut the fish into long strips.

3 Mix the beaten egg with seasoning in a shallow bowl. Put the pretzel crumbs in another shallow bowl. Put all the pieces of fish together into the beaten egg.

4 Lift out each piece of fish one at a time and toss in the crumbs to coat evenly. Lay these on a large plate and chill, uncovered, for about 20 minutes while you make the sauce.

Pretzels

Visitors to the Oktoberfest will remember seeing pretzels in huge baskets being sold by smiling girls moving from table to table in authentic costume. At least, if they remember any of the evening's events, this sight will be among them. This culinary delight is yet another of Bavaria's claims to fame. Pretzels as they are today can only be made by hand, despite attempts to consign the work to machines. The German word 'Brezen' owes its origins to the Latin bracchium, meaning arm; this gives us a clue as to its ultimate origin, with its traditional folded arms shape. But the sweet and salty taste is also used on pretzel rolls and a variety of other baked goods too.

There are many stories concerning the origins of pretzels. One tells how a baker who lived at the foot of the Alps was thrown into prison on a charge of supplying bad bread. The authorities offered to free him if he succeeded in baking a bread through which the sun could shine thrice. After lots of effort and many sleepless nights he came up with the pretzel.

5 Sauté the onion and garlic in the tablespoon of oil and knob of butter for 5 minutes. Stir in the chopped tomatoes, herbs, sugar and seasoning. Bring to the boil then simmer for 15 minutes until reduced.

6 Whizz the mixture in a food processor or blender until smooth. Return to the pan and mix in the Quark. Heat until bubbling, check the seasoning and set aside.

7 Heat enough oil in a deep frying-pan or wok to a depth of about 3 cm (1¼ inch). When it reaches a temperature of 180°C/350°F (or when a small cube of bread browns in half a minute), carefully lower in the fish strips.

8 Fry for about 2 minutes, turning once until crispy and golden. Remove with a slotted spoon and drain on paper towels. Reheat the oil and cook the rest of the fish.

9 Season the crispy fish and serve on a bed of salad leaves with the sauce poured into a jug or bowl. It should not need reheating. Great with chips, pasta or mashed potatoes.

Salmon escalopes with Sauerkraut and green cabbage stir-fry

Lachs mit Sauerkraut und Kohl aus der Pfanne

Fish and Sauerkraut is a popular combination in Germany, particularly using freshwater river and lake fish such as zander and carp. The only freshwater fish easily available in the UK are trout or farmed salmon. For a lighter Sauerkraut flavour, look for Weinkraut which is steeped in white wine. It is very tasty stir-fried with shredded fresh cabbage. Escalopes of salmon are skinless fillets cut across the grain. Serves 4

3 tablespoons rapeseed oil
4 x 120 g (2 oz) fresh salmon escalopes
a small glass of dry white wine
2 teaspoons pickled pink peppercorns
2 tablespoons Quark
sea salt and freshly ground black pepper
a little chopped fresh parsley, to serve

For the stir-fry vegetables:
¼ **fresh green cabbage**
half a 500 g jar Sauerkraut, drained
1 small onion, sliced thinly
½ green pepper, cored and sliced thinly

1 Prepare the vegetables first. Cut the hard central core from the cabbage, and using a large sharp knife shred as finely as possible.

2 Rinse the Sauerkraut in cold water then drain well, squeezing as dry as possible with the back of a ladle. Pat dry with paper towels.

3 Heat 2 tablespoons of the oil in a wok and stir-fry the onion and green pepper for 2 minutes. Add the fresh green cabbage and fry for another 2 minutes, then mix in the Sauerkraut and cook until piping hot. Season well, especially with pepper. Set aside to keep warm.

4 Heat the remaining oil in a large frying-pan. Season the salmon and pan-fry for 3 minutes on the top side until nicely caramelised. Turn over carefully and fry the underside for 2–3 minutes until the flesh feels just firm but not hard.

5 Remove the fish to a warm plate. Pour the wine into the pan along with the pink peppercorns and bubble until reduced by half. Stir in the Quark, season and remove the pan from the heat.

6 Divide the vegetable stir-fry between four warm plates. Place a salmon escalope on top and spoon over the sauce. Sprinkle with some chopped parsley and serve.

Pumpernickel

This Westphalian tradition was once the subject of universal mockery before Prussia's King Frederick William IV ensured its acceptance at the tables of the nobility. Originally baked every fortnight in a long and arduous process of kneading and even treading with feet before baking for up to 24 hours, its chief advantage was that it could be kept for a long time. Another was that the length of time in the oven caramelised the starch in the rye flour to give a dark colour and slight sweetness on the palate. Today the entire process is highly mechanised.

Matjes herrings
Matjes

There are a variety of ready-prepared herring salads in light cream sauce that can be quickly mixed into light and delicious meals. They are sold in packs of 200 g and 400 g, and may contain other ingredients such as chopped apple, onion and dill. Because they have plenty of sauce, there is no need to add extra dressing. Salted matjes are ideal for a quick supper bake.

POTATO PANCAKES WITH MATJES HERRINGS
Reibekuchen mit Matjes

Boil some potatoes in salted water for 10 minutes until they are partly cooked. Drain and rinse under cold water. Grate them coarsely into a bowl and season well. Heat some butter and oil in a large frying-pan and spoon in neat tablespoons of the mixture. Fry over a medium heat until the underside is golden brown – about 3 minutes – then turn and cook the other side. Make sure they are well drained and keep warm, uncovered, to keep them crisp. Place two per portion on a small plate and spoon about a 100 g serving of herring salad on top or by the side. A few crispy leaves of lettuce topped with coarsely grated carrot dressed with poppy seeds makes a good accompaniment.

POTATO, ONION AND MATJES LAYERED SUPPER BAKE
Kartoffel, Zwiebel und Matjes Auflauf

Peel 2 large potatoes and slice thinly with a sharp knife or on a mandolin. Peel and slice a red onion thinly. Drain a 250 g pack of mildly salted Matjes herrings and pat dry. Cut into small pieces. Now layer the potato, onion and herring into a medium-size ovenproof baking dish, dotting the layers with knobs of butter and finishing with a layer of potato. Season with pepper only as herrings are quite salty. Beat 300 ml (½ pint) single cream with 2 medium eggs and slowly pour over the liquid, tapping the dish so the liquid seeps into any gaps. Top with grated Emmenthal cheese and bake at Gas Mark 4/180°C/350°F for 35–45 minutes until the potatoes feel cooked when pierced and the top is golden and bubbling.

Trout fillets in Black Forest ham wraps

Forellenfilets im Schwarz-wälder Schinken-Mantel

Richly flavoured fish such as trout, salmon or mackerel are nicely complemented with a smoky ham flavour and hot piquant sauce. You will need some fresh stock for this, which can be fish, chicken or (surprisingly) beef.
Serves 4

4 fresh trout fillets, about 125 g (4½ oz) each
4 thin slices Black Forest Ham
a little rapeseed oil, for cooking
sea salt and freshly ground black pepper
For the sauce:
½ small onion, sliced
2 tablespoons white wine vinegar
1 bay leaf
2 strips lemon peel
2 whole cloves
1 teaspoon sugar
450 ml (16 fl oz) stock: fish, chicken or beef, preferably homemade
2 teaspoons cornflour
2 tablespoons German mustard
25 g (1 oz) butter
2 free-range egg yolks

1 Make the sauce first. Put the onion, vinegar, bay leaf, lemon peel, cloves, sugar and stock into a saucepan and add some freshly ground pepper. Boil to reduce down by half then strain through a sieve and discard the solids.

2 Return the liquid to the pan. Slake the cornflour with 2 tablespoons cold water. Put the stock back on a simmer and whisk in the slaked cornflour. Simmer until thickened and smooth, then whisk in the mustard and butter.

3 Beat the egg yolks in a medium bowl set on a damp cloth (to hold the bowl steady) and slowly whisk in the hot liquid. Pour back into the pan, and on the lowest heat continue to whisk for a minute or two until the sauce thickens. Immediately remove and pour the sauce back into the bowl so it won't overheat and curdle.

4 For the trout, season the fish fillets. Wrap each fillet in a slice of ham. Place join-side-down in a lightly greased baking dish and brush the ham with a little oil.

5 Heat the oven to Gas Mark 4/180°C/350°F. Bake the fish, uncovered for about 12–15 minutes until it feels firm when pressed. Remove and let it stand for 5 minutes.

6 Reheat the sauce gently. Place a fillet on each of four warmed plates and spoon the sauce around. Serve with parsley, dressed boiled potatoes and some broccoli or green beans.

Fish cakes with green sauce
Fischfrikadellen mit grüner Sauce

Green sauce is one of the great German favourites and is served as an accompaniment to many dishes – boiled beef, sausages, grills and roasts. It is also an excellent sauce for fish. Traditionally, cooks would try and add up to seven types of fresh herbs including, cottage garden herbs such as borage or lovage. If you have to rely on fresh herbs from your local store then just make up what you can. They all blend together surprisingly well. You will need a food processor for this recipe.

Serves 4

2 potatoes, peeled
1 onion, halved
250 g (9 oz) white fish fillets, skinned
150 g (5 oz) smoked fish fillets, skinned
a little flour for dusting
some rapeseed oil for shallow frying
sea salt and freshly ground black pepper
For the sauce:
about 60 g (2 oz) mixture of fresh green
    herbs: choose from parsley, chives,
    chervil, dill, marjoram, sorrel,
    coriander, basil, tarragon, borage,
    lovage, rocket or baby spinach.
    (Use more pungent herbs sparingly.)
3 tablespoons Quark
2 tablespoons milk
2 tablespoons mayonnaise
2 teaspoons sweet German mustard
2 hard-boiled eggs, chopped roughly

1 Coarsely grate the potatoes and squeeze out excess water. Coarsely grate the onion – mix half into the potato and reserve half for the sauce.

2 Check both fish for fine bones then chop roughly and place in a food processor with some freshly ground black pepper. Whizz to a smooth paste then scoop out and mix with the grated potato and onion. Add a little salt if liked – you can check the seasoning by frying a small amount first. Shape into 8 round cakes.

3 Make the sauce. Wash out the processor and blend your chosen mixture of herbs until finely chopped. Add the rest of the ingredients including the reserved onion, chopped eggs and seasoning to taste.

4 Whizz to a slightly chunky purée – not velvety smooth, it should have a little texture. Check the seasoning and spoon into a bowl.

5 Dust the fish cakes lightly with flour. Heat some oil to a depth of 1 cm (½ inch) and fry the fish cakes in batches for about 3 minutes each side on a medium heat. Drain on paper towels and reheat the oil between the batches. Serve the fish cakes with the sauce and a fresh tomato salad.

Brightly coloured Easter eggs. These are first dyed and then the pattern is etched into the colour

Easter eggs

Hot wax, goose feathers, knives and files, salt and even fire are all used to decorate the famous Easter eggs that are a tradition in many parts of Germany today. The brightly coloured, hard boiled eggs are hidden in the gardens in little nests of green wool. Sweets are placed with them and on Easter Sunday the children are sent into the garden to find them.

Meat
and Poultry

There is no doubting the popularity of meat dishes in Germany, from Schnitzels to meatballs and marinated slow-cooked Sauerbraten. Beef, veal, poultry and game find their way onto millions of plates each day but pork is by far the most popular meat, both served fresh as stews and steaks, or cured as Kasseler, sausages and Katenspeck. The one feature that unifies all meat dishes is the use of top quality meat. No self-respecting German cook would consider cooking anything less.

Above: grilled Kasseler with Sauerkraut, fried apple slices and parsley-coated potatoes.

Kasseler steaks with pineapple and juniper Sauerkraut

Kasseler mit Ananaskraut

Serves 4

500 g jar Sauerkraut
1 onion, chopped
3 tablespoons rapeseed oil
125 g fresh or unsweetened canned
   pineapple chunks
1 teaspoon juniper berries, crushed
300 ml (½ pint) ham or chicken stock
4 x 100 g Kasseler steaks
15 g (½ oz) butter
2 tablespoons chopped fresh parsley
sea salt and freshly ground black pepper

1 Drain the Sauerkraut and rinse in a colander under cold water. Press down well to drain. In a large saucepan, sauté the onion in 2 tablespoons of oil for 5 minutes then stir in the pineapple, Sauerkraut, juniper berries, stock and seasoning. Bring to a boil, then partially cover and simmer for 20 minutes, stirring occasionally.

2 Meanwhile, heat the remaining tablespoon of oil in a large frying-pan and fry the steaks for about 7 minutes on each side. Season with pepper only. Remove and stand for 5 minutes.

3 Stir the butter and parsley into the Sauerkraut and serve alongside the Kasseler steaks. Serve with potatoes coated in parsley butter.

Kasseler

Necessity is again the mother of invention with Kasseler. Despite the name it's not from the German town, Kassel, but is the result of experiments in conserving pork by a certain Herr Cassel from Berlin's Potsdamer Street. The result – a distinctive smoked and cured pork – is one of the most popular pork products eaten in Germany today. It is often paired with Sauerkraut.

Honey mustard Kasseler and green leaf salad

Grüner Salat mit Kasseler Streifen

This is a quick, light bistro-style dish ideal for mid-week suppers and so healthy! Use whatever mixture you like of green salad leaves but a base of torn iceberg and baby spinach would be nice. Some food halls sell packs of German croûtons flavoured in many ways. I suggest you use the herb croûtons for this dish and steaks of lean loin Kasseler.

Serves 4

**250 g (9 oz) mixture green salad leaves –
choose from iceberg, spinach, frisée,
oak-leaf, lamb's lettuce and rocket etc.**
**½ cucumber, halved, de-seeded and
sliced thinly**
1 large carrot, grated coarsely
**3–4 tablespoons coarsely grated celeriac
tossed in lemon juice**
1 punnet of mustard and cress, snipped
4 x 100 g lean loin Kasseler steaks
1 tablespoon rapeseed oil
2 teaspoons clear German flower honey
**1 tablespoon coarse-grain German
mustard**
**4 tablespoons Basic Oil and Vinegar
Dressing (page 22)**
half 100 g pack herb croûtons (optional)
sea salt and freshly ground black pepper

1 Tear any large salad leaves into bite-size pieces. Wash and dry any leaves if necessary. Place in a large mixing bowl with the cucumber 'moons', carrot, celeriac and cress. Season and set aside.

2 Cook the Kasseler in the oil for about 5–7 minutes on each side until just tender. Remove and cut each steak into 5–6 strips. Meanwhile, stir honey and mustard into the pan. When hot toss in the Kasseler strips to coat evenly.

3 Toss the salad with the dressing and croûtons (if used) and divide between four plates. Scatter over the Kasseler strips and serve immediately.

Pork and beer stew

Schweinefleisch- und Bier-Eintopf

In several parts of Germany, breadcrumbs are used to thicken soups and stews, a brilliant idea that adds a delicious rich and slightly nutty flavour especially when beer is used instead of stock. This recipe uses shoulder of pork but it works equally well with beef or veal, and is a wonderful warming winter casserole. Serve this with buttered cabbage or kale and potato dumplings, mashed potatoes or fresh Spätzle (see page 68).

Serves 4

600 g (1 lb 5 oz) braising pork, e.g. lean
    shoulder, cubed
2 tablespoons rapeseed oil
1 large onion, sliced
2 garlic cloves, crushed
2 carrots, cut in chunky sticks
125 g (4½ oz) brown button mushrooms,
    sliced (optional)
¼ teaspoon ground allspice
1 large bay leaf
1 small cinnamon stick
500 ml bottle dark Bavarian wheat beer
75 g (2¾ oz) fresh rye bread made into
    crumbs
sea salt and freshly ground black pepper
chopped fresh parsley, to serve

1 In a large heavy-based saucepan, brown the pork in half the oil for about 5 minutes until nicely browned. Remove with a slotted spoon.

2 Add the remaining oil and sauté the onion and garlic for another 5 minutes, until softened.

3 Stir in the carrots, mushrooms if used and cook for 5 minutes, then add the spices and bay leaf. Return the meat to the pan, stir in the beer and mix in the breadcrumbs.

4 Season, then bring to the boil, stirring once or twice. Make sure the meat is pressed under the liquid, then partially cover and simmer very gently for about an hour.

5 Uncover, remove the bay leaf and cinnamon stick. Sprinkle with parsley to serve.

Wheat beer

Today German wheat beer is the latest trendy offering in drinking holes everywhere; combining the refreshing zest of lager with the complexities of ale, this 'champagne of the beer world' is fast catching on. Using an unusual combination of both barley and wheat malt (at least 50%) the final pale colouring is matched with a smell and taste of fruit and spice. It was very popular during the 17th and early 18th centuries, but fell from grace in the 19th century because of a wheat shortage. There are three types available; dark, clear and filtered, or cloudy with yeast.

Beef Sauerbraten

Rheinischer Sauerbraten

A classic dish originally from the Rhineland, Sauerbraten is a lean, slow-roasting joint of beef marinated in a sweet-sour mixture then braised in the oven. Some recipes have the sauce thickened with gingerbread crumbs and further sweetened with plump raisins. The fruit and meat theme is continued with accompaniments – apple sauce and sweetened carrots. A good joint for a lazy Sunday lunch. Serve with boiled potatoes or potato pancakes.
Serves 6

For the marinade:
1 large onion, quartered
4 cloves
a good pinch of allspice
2 carrots, sliced
2 large bay leaves
1 tablespoon medium-hot German
    mustard
300 ml (½ pint) red wine vinegar
For the main dish:
1.2 kg (2¼ lb) lean slow-roast beef joint,
    boned and rolled, e.g. silverside,
    topside, brisket etc.
2 tablespoons rapeseed oil
1 large onion, sliced
100 g (3½ oz) Katenspeck, de-rinded
    and chopped
a small glass of red wine
3 tablespoons raisins
sea salt and ground black pepper

1 The beef needs to marinate first for 3–4 days in the fridge. Stick the cloves into the onion quarters then place with all the marinade ingredients in a saucepan with 500 ml (18 fl oz) water. Boil for 2 minutes then cool to room temperature.

2 Put the beef into a deep dish with room enough for the marinade. Alternatively, put the beef into a large thick plastic bag. Pour in the marinade, including vegetables and spices. Cover or seal and chill for 3–4 days, turning the meat or shaking the bag every day.

3 Remove the meat and pat dry. Strain the marinade and set aside. Heat the oil in a large frying-pan and brown the meat all over. Remove the meat, add the sliced onion and Katenspeck. Sauté for about 5 minutes until softened.

4 Replace the meat on top of the onion mix. Pour in a quarter of the marinade, bring to the boil then cover and simmer on the lowest heat for about 1 hour.

5 Add the red wine, return to a simmer, cover again and cook for another 30–40 minutes until the meat is nice and tender. Remove from the pan and set aside to stand before cutting into slices.

6 Boil the pan juices down to about 300 ml (½ pint), season and strain into a smaller pan with the raisins. Simmer for 5 minutes then serve with the meat.

German apple sauce

Peel, core and chop about 500 g (1 lb 2 oz) German Jonagold or Rubinette apples. Simmer with a small glass of water, 3 tablespoons caster sugar, 1 tablespoon fresh lemon juice and a whole clove until softened, but still with a chunky texture – about 5 minutes. Stir in a knob of butter and cool.

Holstein Schnitzel
Schnitzel nach Holsteiner Art

This recipe was the favourite meal of the great 19th-century Prussian diplomat Friedrich von Holstein – who liked to eat in a hurry – so had his starters and main course all on one plate. It certainly makes an attractive presentation, although it is best to serve it on large plates! Pork fillets could be used instead of veal.
Serves 4

4 steaks of veal fillet, about 125 g (4½ oz) each
100 g (3½ oz) butter
some rapeseed oil for frying
3–4 slices white bread, crusts removed
4 medium free-range eggs
2 slices smoked salmon, halved
4 anchovy fillets, rinsed and dried
4 sardines or sprats in oil, patted dry
2 tablespoons capers, drained,
**   or 3 gherkins, chopped**
chopped fresh parsley
sea salt and freshly ground black pepper

1 If the veal fillets are thick, place them between 2 sheets of baking parchment and beat with a rolling pin to flatten.

2 Have a warm oven at the ready. Fry the veal in two batches. Heat a quarter of the butter with a little oil until it stops foaming then quickly add 2 fillets. Fry for about 2 minutes on each side until lightly browned and just tender. Season in the pan then remove and keep warm. Repeat with another quarter of butter, a trickle of oil and the last 2 fillets.

3 Cut the bread into triangles. Melt the remaining butter with another spoon of oil and when it is hot fry the bread triangles quickly on each side until browned and crisp. Drain on paper towels.

4 Wipe out the pan if it needs it and heat about a tablespoon of oil, then fry the eggs two at a time, sunny side up. Season and drain.

5 Now you can put the dish together on four large warmed plates. Top four of the fried croûtes with a half slice of smoked salmon, four with an anchovy curled to fit and four with a sardine or sprat, cut in half. Sprinkle them with parsley and grind over some pepper.

6 Place the croûtes on the edge of the plates with the veal in the centre. Slide an egg on each veal fillet, scatter with the capers or gherkins and eat quickly in the style of von Holstein!

Crusty pork loin with rhubarb and celery Sauerkraut

Schweinebraten mit Rhabarber und Selleriesauerkraut

The Viktualienmarkt Munich – this famous food market sells many high-quality traditional German products

Pork has to be Germany's national meat. Apart from all the sausages and smoked cured meats, fresh pork is cooked in many ways, often partnered with varieties of Sauerkraut. Tart fruits such as apples are good matches as is rhubarb. Serve the meat carved in thick slices accompanied by potato dumplings (see page 78).

Serves 6

1 pork loin joint, on the bone, about 1.5 kg (3 lb) rind well scored
½ teaspoon caraway seeds, crushed
1 teaspoon salt
sea salt and freshly ground black pepper
For the Sauerkraut:
500 g jar Sauerkraut
4 sticks pink rhubarb, cut into chunks
1 tablespoon caster sugar
2 tablespoons rapeseed oil
1 onion, sliced
2 sticks celery, sliced thinly
50 g (1¾ oz) Katenspeck, chopped
2 tablespoons flour
200 ml (7 fl oz) chicken or vegetable stock
3 tablespoons soured cream
some chopped fresh parsley
sea salt and freshly ground black pepper

1 Heat the oven to Gas Mark 6/200°C/400°F. At the same time, heat a large empty frying-pan until very hot. Holding the pork loin in a clean tea towel to protect your hand, press the rind down onto the hot metal and hold for as long as you can, rolling the rind to make sure it all seals. When golden brown, remove and pat the top dry with a paper towel. This helps the rind to roast to a crisp crackling.

2 Place the joint in a roasting pan. Mix the crushed caraway seeds with a teaspoon of salt and sprinkle over the joint, rubbing it into the sides as well.

3 Roast for 30 minutes, without basting, then turn the temperature down to Gas Mark 4/180°C/350°F and cook for another 30–40 minutes until the juices run clear when the centre is pierced. A meat thermometer should give a reading of 85–90°C.

4 Meanwhile, cook the Sauerkraut. First, drain the Sauerkraut and rinse in a colander under cold water. Drain again.

5 Heat a large heavy-based saucepan until very hot. Toss the rhubarb with the sugar and quickly stir it into the pan. It should caramelise nicely. Remove and set aside. Wipe out the pan and add the oil. Sauté the onion, celery and Katenspeck for about 5 minutes until softened.

6 Mix in the flour and cook for a minute or two then stir in the stock until bubbling. Add the Sauerkraut, season and cook for 15 minutes.

7 Add the caramelised rhubarb, return to a gentle simmer and continue cooking for another ten minutes or so. Stir into the soured cream and parsley. Check the seasoning and set aside.

8 When the pork is ready, allow it to rest for 10 minutes then remove the crackling and break into chunks. Carve the meat into medium thick slices and pour over any roasting juices, but not the fat. Serve the meat with the Sauerkraut and top with the crackling.

Roast chicken with blue brie
Hähnchen mit Blauschimmelbrie

A delicious German variation on a simple roast chicken dinner. Slip slices of creamy blue brie under the breast skin and serve with little grilled Nuremberg sausages wrapped in thin slices of Katenspeck or Black Forest ham. The pan juices can be made into a light creamy sauce. Serves 4

1 large roasting chicken, about 2 kg (4 lb)
150 g (5 oz) Bavarian blue brie, de-rinded
a little rapeseed oil
2 sprigs fresh tarragon, thyme or
**   rosemary**
8 small Nuremberg sausages
4 thin slices Katenspeck, halved
**   widthways**
a small glass of dry white wine
2–3 tablespoons double cream
sea salt and freshly ground black pepper

1 Heat the oven to Gas Mark 4/180°C/350°F. Untruss the chicken, pull out the inner cavity pad of fat and work your fingers under the breast skin to loosen it.

2 Cut the cheese into three slices. Push a slice under the skin of each breast.

3 Place the chicken in a roasting pan and brush the skin with a little oil. Season and scatter the leaves from your chosen herb sprigs on top. Roast for 1 hour, checking to see the breast meat doesn't over-brown. If it does then cover with a butter paper or some foil. Check the chicken is done by piercing the thigh – the juices should run clear. If not, cook for a further 10 minutes or so.

4 Meanwhile, wrap the sausages in the halved Speck and brush lightly with more oil. Place in a roasting pan and cook for the last 20 minutes or so of roasting.

5 When the chicken is cooked, remove from the pan and allow to stand. It will keep hot for a good 15 minutes or so.

6 Place the roasting pan on the hob and deglaze with the wine, scraping up any meaty pieces. When the wine has bubbled down by half add a small glass of water (or some boiling water from any vegetables you are cooking to accompany). Stir the pan well and mix in the cream. Finally, drop chunks of the last slice of brie into the hot liquid and stir until melted. Season and strain into a sauce boat.

7 Carve the bird into four servings and allow 2 wrapped sausages per serving. Serve with sautéed or plain boiled potatoes.

Turkey fillets with pepper brie and Black Forest ham
Truthahn-Cordon-Bleu

Turkey is a popular meat throughout the year in Germany, not just associated with Christmas time. This is a quick and easy meal, ideal for mid-week eating. Buy two large turkey breasts for four people and use the lean, cured Black Forest ham to enclose the creamy brie stuffing. Serves 4

2 whole boneless turkey breasts, skinned,
**   about 300 g (10½ oz) each**
150 g (5 oz) German brie with
**   peppercorns**
4 large or 6 medium sized slices Black
**   Forest ham**
150 g (5½ oz) button mushrooms, sliced

1 tablespoon rapeseed oil
25 g (1 oz) butter
a small glass of dry white wine
2–3 tablespoons double cream
sea salt and freshly ground black pepper

1 Cut each turkey breast in half horizontally, but don't cut quite all the way through. Open out the breast like a book, so it lays flat. Slice the rind off the cheese and cut into four slices.

2 Season the meat and press two slices of cheese and half the ham on each breast. Reshape, enclosing the cheese and ham entirely.

3 Preheat the oven to Gas Mark 5/ 190°C/375°F. Sauté the mushrooms in the oil and butter for 5 minutes, until softened. Season and place on the base of a small roasting pan. Lay the turkey on top.

4 Cover loosely with a butter paper or lightly greased sheet of foil and bake for 20–25 minutes until the meat feels firm. A little cheese may have seeped out.

5 Remove the turkey to a warm plate and let stand. Place the roasting pan and mushrooms on the hob and pour in the wine. Bubble down until reduced by half then stir in the cream. Season.

6 Cut the wrapped turkey breasts into four diagonal slices each. Transfer these to four warmed plates, spoon the mushroom sauce over and serve. Particularly good with homemade Spätzle (see page 68), which can be made ahead then reheated in butter with chopped parsley.

Roast goose with liver paté stuffing and redcurrant glazed peaches

Gänsebraten mit Leberwurstklößchen und glasierten Pfirsichen

The first goose of the season is eaten on 11 November, St Martin's Day, and it's the traditional German Christmas dish. Roast goose frequently appears on menus all over Germany. Its dark, delicious and tender meat cooks to a light crispness on the outside while the rich skin means the flesh bastes itself. Cook tasty liver paté and rye breadcrumb stuffing balls alongside and, for a special serving, add halved fresh peaches baked and glazed with sugar and redcurrants. (If your butcher or supermarket cannot supply a goose, check through mail-order sources. Many producers will supply one direct.)

Serves 6

1 whole oven-ready goose, about 3½–4 kg (7–8 lb) weight
3 large just-ripe peaches, halved and stoned
40 g (1½ oz) butter, melted
a small punnet of fresh redcurrants
2 tablespoons light brown sugar
some good pinches of ground cinnamon
1–2 tablespoons plain flour
300 ml (½ pint) stock or water
2 tablespoons redcurrant jam
a little fresh lemon juice
sea salt and freshly ground black pepper

For the stuffing:

1 small onion, chopped

1 tablespoon rapeseed oil + extra for brushing stuffing balls

½ teaspoon ground paprika

½ teaspoon dried sage

grated zest of 1 small lemon

100 g (3½ oz) German calves' liver paté, softened

150 g (5½ oz) fresh rye breadcrumbs

½ teaspoon sea salt

1 medium free-range egg, beaten

1 Heat the oven to Gas Mark 5/190°C/375°F. Prick the skin of the goose in several places, especially around the leg and thigh. Rub the breast with salt. Place on a raised trivet set inside a roasting dish.

2 Roast for about 1½ hours, lowering the temperature to Gas Mark 3/170°C/320°F if the bird starts to over-brown.

3 For the peaches, brush them with melted butter and place in another shallow roasting dish. Strip the redcurrants from the stalks and mix with the sugar. Spoon into the peach cavities and dust with cinnamon. Bake them on the shelf above the goose at the start of the roasting for 15-20 minutes then remove and cool to room temperature.

4 Meanwhile, make the stuffing. Sauté the onion in the oil for 5 minutes then stir in the paprika and cook for half a minute. Cool then mix with the rest of the stuffing ingredients adding pepper to taste. Shape into 6 balls using wet hands if necessary.

5 Lay them in a shallow ovenproof dish, brush with oil and bake for the last 30 minutes of roasting, near the top of the oven. As the goose cooks, you may want to pour off the fat as it drips off to cut down on it smoking. Make sure you have help to do this, as the bird will be heavy.

6 When the goose has cooked, remove and stand for 10 minutes before carving. Pour the fat off the pan and sprinkle in the flour. Stir well and cook for a minute then pour in about 300 ml (½ pint) stock or vegetable water. Stir well and boil, then add 2 tablespoons redcurrant jam, a squeeze of fresh lemon juice and seasoning.

7 Strain into a jug, then after the bird has been carved, pour the juices over. Arrange the stuffing balls and peaches around. It should look very inviting.

The Christchild's market in Nuremberg

Leberkäse

This Bavarian meat loaf is not only a dish for all seasons but for all times of day too. From lunch through to supper there are variations and accompaniments which make it a very versatile food. Served in a bun, it's the Bavarian answer to the burger. Fresh from the oven, it's delicious thickly sliced with mustard, and another favourite is to top it with a fried egg and eat it with traditional potato salad. Don't be fooled by the German name Leberkäse; there's no liver and no cheese in it either, just good lean pork and beef.

Pot roast pheasant with creamy Sauerkraut and red onion

Gebratener Fasan mit Sauerkraut und roten Zwiebeln

Game birds are becoming easier to buy now in UK supermarkets – not only pheasants but also guinea fowl, pigeons, partridges and even tiny quails. They all suit slow pot roasting and are ideal for Sauerkraut which can be embellished in a number of different ways.
Serves 4

2 oven-ready pheasants, about 1 kg (2lb) each
50 g (1¾ oz) butter
some thin strips of Katenspeck, to cover the breasts
250 ml (9 fl oz) red wine
sea salt and freshly ground black pepper
For the Sauerkraut mixture:
1 red onion, sliced
1 tablespoon rapeseed oil
1 teaspoon juniper berries, lightly crushed
a pinch of allspice
1 fresh thyme sprig
1 bay leaf
500 g jar Sauerkraut or Weinkraut, drained
3–4 tablespoons double cream

1 Untruss the birds, if necessary. Wash the body cavities of the pheasants and pat dry. Place in a shallow casserole dish, dot the breasts with half the butter and season well. Preheat the oven to Gas Mark 6/200°C/400°F and roast the birds for about 10 minutes to start the skin browning.

2 Cover the breasts with strips of Katenspeck to protect them in cooking, pour in two-thirds of the wine then cover and return to the oven. Reduce the heat to Gas Mark 4/180°C/350°F and cook for about 45 minutes, basting twice during the cooking and re-covering each time.

3 Meanwhile, make the Sauerkraut mixture. Sauté the onion in the oil for 5 minutes until softened. Then add the juniper, allspice, thyme, bay leaf, Sauerkraut and remaining wine. Season, bring to a simmer then cook for 20 minutes.

4 Uncover and bubble down to reduce the liquid by half then mix in the cream.

5 Back to the birds. Remove them and allow to rest for 10 minutes. Put the strips of Speck back into the pan plus any resting juices from the bird. Bubble up on the hob for a minute or two, season and whisk in the remaining butter. Strain into a small pan and keep warm.

6 Cut the birds into half, using poultry shears, and remove the breasts whole. Slice each into three. Cut off the thighs and legs. Spoon the Sauerkraut onto four warmed plates. Place a thigh and leg joint on top then the breast slices. Pour over the red wine gravy and serve

Roast venison with a ragoût of forest mushrooms

Rehbraten mit Waldpilzragout

Germany has a long tradition of hunting, especially in the forests of the south in the majestic region of Bavaria. Speciality game butchers treat shoppers to beautiful displays of perfectly prepared ready-to-cook joints or casserole meat. Venison is a popular choice. Accompaniments could include braised red cabbage, a redcurrant and onion relish or this mixture of fragrant wild mushrooms enriched in a sweet mustard cream sauce. You will need a larding needle to thread the strips of fatty Speck.
Serves 6

boned fillet or haunch joint of venison, about 1.2 kg (2½ lb)
200 g (7 oz) piece fat Speck
a little rapeseed oil for browning
sea salt and freshly ground black pepper
For the mushroom ragoût:
300–400 g (10–14 oz) fresh wild mushrooms – e.g. ceps, oyster mushrooms, girolles, morels etc.
1 onion, sliced
1 fat garlic clove, crushed
50 g (1¾ oz) Katenspeck, de-rinded and chopped
2 tablespoons rapeseed oil
25 g (1 oz) butter
a good pinch of dried thyme or marjoram
a small glass of dry white wine
2 tablespoons German sweet mustard
4 tablespoons crème fraîche or double cream

1 Trim the venison, if necessary, to a neat shape. Cut the fat Speck into long strips 1 cm (½-inch) wide. Clamp the strips, one at a time, between the grip of the larding needle and pull through the length of the joint. Repeat this with as many of the strips as will fit. Any scraps of

Speck can be scattered on the top of the joint for roasting. Preheat the oven to Gas Mark 4/180°C/350°F. Tie the joint in a neat shape with kitchen string.

2 Heat a little oil in a large frying-pan. When hot, brown the joint all over, then remove and place in a roasting pan. Season, scatter any spare pieces of Speck on top to baste the joint and roast for about 1–1¼ hours until the meat feels just firm and very slightly springy, that is, medium rare. If you have a meat thermometer, the internal temperature should read 65°C.

3 Meanwhile, make the mushroom ragoût. Pick over the mushrooms and clean if necessary, although try not to wash them as this makes them go slimy. Cut into slices.

4 Sauté the onion, garlic and Katenspeck in the oil for about 5 minutes until softened. Add the butter, raise the heat and mix in the mushrooms, stirring quickly until they are all well sealed. Season, then add the herbs. Pour in the wine. Cook rapidly until reduced by half.

5 Stir in the mustard and finally the cream. Bring to a gentle simmer for a minute or two, check the seasoning and set aside until the venison is cooked.

6 When the venison is ready, remove it from the oven, discard any Speck pieces on top and allow to rest for 10 minutes. It will stay hot. Cut the venison into thick slices. Spoon the mushrooms onto a warmed platter, arrange the venison on top and trickle over any juices from the roasting pan and carving board.

Many Bavarian villages have a tall pole such as this one bearing brightly coloured images of the different crafts which are carried on in the village and showing the regional costume

Sauerkraut seller. He is selling Sauerkraut fresh out of the tub in which it has been fermented

The main vegetables used in pickles are cucumbers (in various sizes), cabbages (red and white), celeriac, carrots, peppers and cauliflower. Pickles can be steeped in mild and sweetened vinegar or brine and are flavoured with aromatic spices and seeds. Mustard is the perfect partner for smoked and cured meats and sausages, and there is a variety of strengths and flavours on offer. But Germany's most famous pickle – Sauerkraut – also doubles as a vegetable accompaniment to be served in hot and cold dishes.

Germans are particularly fond of pickles, relishes and mustards to complement and enhance their meals

Pickles

RED CABBAGE (Rotkohl) Sold in cans or jars, shredded Rotkohl has many uses at the dining table. It has been prepared in an apple-flavoured, sweet-sour pickle and retains its attractive deep red colour and crisp texture. It is a classic side dish for roast pork, duck, goose and game.

MUSTARD CUCUMBER (Senfgurken) In this pickle brown and yellow mustard seeds are added to yellow gherkins.

MIXED PICKLES (Sauer eingelegtes Gemüse) A brightly coloured medley of crisp and tasty pickled vegetables.

SAUERKRAUT This is thinly shredded white cabbage salted and left to ferment for weeks to develop a unique piquant flavour.

CELERIAC SALAD Julienne strips of a mild celery-flavoured root vegetable blanched and with a mild vinegar dressing.

MUSTARD (Senf) Mixed with vinegar, salt, spices and sugar, German mustards are very aromatic.

CORNICHONS Baby pickled gherkins are suitable for a host of meal occasions.

CREAMED HORSERADISH (Meerrettich) Good with hams and sliced cold meats, for hot roast beef and even crispy fried fish.

PICKLED PEPPER SALAD (Paprikasalat) This relish is bound to enhance many buffet tables and cold meat platters.

SWEET MUSTARD (Süsser Senf) Unique to Germany. Popular with those who enjoy a gentle piquant dressing.

PICKLED GHERKINS German gherkins are crunchy and firm. Buy them whole or ready sliced – ideal for slipping on top of burgers.

HOT HORSERADISH Serve with roast beef and smoked cured salmon and eel. Mellow enough not to bring tears to your eyes.

CARROT SALAD Include on a buffet table. Popular with children and adults alike. A real family favourite.

Suppers

With our hectic lifestyles, there is less opportunity for families to sit down to meals together. The need for wholesome, light dishes becomes greater. A light main course with perhaps a side salad and a slice or two of crusty bread is often all we feel like eating. Cheese, eggs, bread, Speck and Sauerkraut make excellent bases for such meals. Why not try your hand at making the fastest fresh pasta ever – Spätzle (see page 68) or how about grated potato pancakes which can be made in less time than it takes to peel, boil and mash a pan of potatoes?

Above: Sautéed potatoes with Katenspeck.

Baby tarts of blue cheese

Blauschimmelbrie, Lauch und Sauerkraut-Törtchen

These make a light simple lunch with a mixed salad, or an unusual starter. Use a blue-veined soft cheese such as blue brie. Ideal for vegetarians. Makes 6 tartlets

500 g ready-made shortcrust pastry, thawed if frozen
2 leeks, washed and sliced thinly
2 tablespoons rapeseed oil
half 500 g jar Sauerkraut, drained and rinsed
250 g (9 oz) Bavarian blue brie, crumbled or diced
a scant teaspoon caraway or cumin seeds
1 large free-range egg
2 free-range egg yolks
250 ml (9 fl oz) milk
sea salt and freshly ground black pepper

1 Roll out the pastry to the thickness of a £1 coin. Cut out six 12 cm (5-inch) rounds and fit into six 10 cm (4-inch) tartlet tins or Yorkshire pudding tins. Press the dough rounds well into the sides to make sure they come up beyond the tin edges to allow for shrinkage.

2 Line the tart cases with foil and baking beans and chill for 20 minutes.

3 Sauté the leeks in the oil for 5 minutes until softened. Season and cool. Preheat the oven to Gas Mark 6/200°C/400°F.

4 Bake the tart cases for 10 minutes then remove the foil and beans and bake for another 5 minutes. Reduce the oven to Gas Mark 4/180°C/350°F.

5 Divide the leeks between the tartlet cases and spoon in the Sauerkraut. Drop in the crumbled or diced cheese. Sprinkle over the caraway or cumin seeds.

6 Beat the egg, yolks, milk and seasoning and slowly pour into the four tarts, forking the mixtures together. Return to the oven and bake for 20 minutes until risen and golden brown. Cool before removing from the tins. Serve warm.

Farmer's omelette
Bauern-Omelette

If you have some eggs, a little Katenspeck, cooked potatoes and grilling cheese you can rustle up a great light meal in next to no time. Serves 2–4 depending on appetites

100 g (3½ oz) Katenspeck, chopped
1–2 tablespoons rapeseed oil
1 large Bierwurst
about 200–300 g (7–10 oz) cold cooked
    potatoes
a handful of ready-made croûtons
    (optional)
5 large free-range eggs (size 1–2), beaten
    and seasoned
50 g (1¾ oz) Bavarian Emmenthal, grated
sea salt and freshly ground black pepper

1 Using a medium-size heavy-based non-stick frying-pan, fry the Katenspeck in a tablespoon of oil until crisp. Remove. Drain on paper towel.

2 Halve the sausage lengthways. Slice thickly on the diagonal. Fry the slices until lightly coloured and crisp. Remove and drain.

3 Slice the potatoes to a medium thickness. Heat the remaining oil in the same pan and sauté the potatoes until golden brown, turning once or twice.

4 Return the Katenspeck and sausage to the pan and scatter in the croûtons (if used). Stir everything to mix then slowly pour in the beaten eggs, stirring lightly and tipping the pan

so the liquid egg settles evenly in the pan.

5 Scatter over the cheese and fork lightly in. Turn the heat right down and cook very slowly for 12–15 minutes until the top is lightly set. If you prefer, you could preheat the grill and lightly cook the top until browned.

6 Remove the pan from the heat and allow to stand for 5 minutes before cutting into quarters. Ease out with a palette knife. Serve with a light green salad and crusty bread.

Sausage stalls

The traditional German sausage stall (Wurstbude) is where you can sample a variety of hot sausages. What's on offer will vary from region to region, but is likely to include Frankfurters, Regensburgers and Bratwurst. The sausage stall was once the only surviving hope that the whole world would not one day be swamped with burger bars. The original stall was established in Regensburg in the 12th century, and eight hundred years' practice means that for variety and taste this more traditional fast food wins every time. Just be prepared to miss it when you're back home again!

Outdoor café

Potato pancakes with Katenspeck and cheese

Reibekuchen mit Katenspeck und Käse

Raw grated potato makes a quick and simple 'batter' for pancakes. You can add whatever flavour variations appeal to you, but chopped crispy Katenspeck, grated onion and cheese are always popular. Children in particular will appreciate these – they are certainly a lot more wholesome than packet burgers and fish fingers. For a traditional country flavour, fry the potatoes in a little lard or render down a little fat Speck first.
Serves 4

1 kg (2¼ lb) firm potatoes e.g. Maris Piper
    or Desirée, peeled
1 small onion, grated
2–3 tablespoons flour
½ teaspoon salt
1 tablespoon chopped fresh parsley
leaves from 1 sprig of fresh thyme,
    chopped
100 g (3½ oz) Katenspeck, chopped
75 g (2¾ oz) mountain cheese or
    Emmenthal cheese, grated coarsely
either 40 g (1½ oz) lard or 2–3 tablespoons
    rapeseed oil
sea salt and freshly ground black pepper

1 Coarsely grate the potato and squeeze dry either with your hands or in a colander, pressing down with the back of a ladle.

2 Place in a bowl with the grated onion and mix in the flour. Add half a teaspoon of salt, some freshly ground black pepper and the herbs.

3 In a large non-stick frying-pan, fry the Katenspeck until crisp then remove. Leave the bacon fat in the pan.

4 Stir the Katenspeck into the potato mix along with the cheese. Heat a small knob of lard or a tablespoon of oil with the bacon fat. When hot, drop in a tablespoon of potato and flatten with the back of a spoon to a round shape, or as neatly as you can.

5 Fry for 2–3 minutes over a medium heat until golden brown, then flip over and cook the other side. Repeat with the mixture in batches, say two or three at a time. Top up the fat or oil and make sure it is hot before continuing to fry.

6 Drain on paper towels and keep uncovered in a warm oven while you make the rest of the pancakes. Eat them as they are.

Variation
You could substitute 3 tablespoons of drained Sauerkraut for the grated cheese.

Potato pancakes

Potato pancakes are a traditional Rheinland confection. Once it was mother who wielded the pan; increasingly nowadays special days in bars and cafés are the ideal opportunity to sample this dish, and there are street stalls selling them. The most famous is outside Cologne railway station, so visitors have no excuse not to sample this delicacy! Potato pancakes go by many names in different parts of Germany, for example Reibekuchen and Kartoffelpuffer. They are sometimes served with apple sauce.

Homemade Spätzle
Hausgemachte Spätzle

German cooks have made flour and egg dough noodles for almost as long as the Italians, except their recipes are easier to mix and shape!

Called Spätzle, traditionally the soft dough is spread on a board and then shaved into a pan of boiling water using a sharp knife, which can be a slightly tricky technique to master. There is, however, a simpler method that is just as good and involves rubbing the very soft dough through a flat slotted plate or colander using a spatula or ladle. Almost as soon as the little dough squiggles float to the surface of the water they are cooked. It is that fast and easy.
Serves 4

300 g (10 oz) plain flour
1 teaspoon salt
3 medium free-range eggs, beaten
about 3 tablespoons cold water

1 Sift the flour and salt into a large bowl. Make a well in the centre, tip in the eggs and gradually beat them into the flour with a wooden spoon. As the dough gets thicker add the water gradually until you have a soft, just-runny dough.

2 Bring a large pan of salted water to the boil. Take a small cupful of the soft dough and either rub through a flat Spätzle disc with a plastic spatula or rub through a colander with the back of a ladle. The dough will fall into the water as thick 'squiggles'. They cook very quickly - when they rise to the surface of the water allow them a few seconds longer then scoop out with a slotted spoon into another colander.

3 If cooking ahead, then drop the cooked Spätzle in iced water for a couple of minutes. Otherwise, dress with a little melted butter and seasoning.

Variations
For green herb Spätzle, add 2–3 tablespoons finely chopped fresh herbs to the flour before mixing.

For cheese Spätzle, dress hot cooked Spätzle with melted butter and toss with a little grated German Emmenthal cheese. Sprinkle with freshly grated nutmeg and top with fried browned onion rings.

For Spätzle with fresh tomato sauce, skin, de-seed and chop three large tomatoes. Sauté in 2 tablespoons olive oil with two crushed garlic cloves until you have a rough purée. Season and stir in chopped fresh parsley or shredded basil. Makes a delicious quick and light homemade pasta dish. Top with grated Emmenthal or mountain cheese.

Courgette and mushroom Quark bake

Zucchini-Pilzauflauf mit Quark

Quark makes a good light baked topping when mixed with beaten eggs and this dish is nice to serve for a family supper.
Serves 4

3 tablespoons rapeseed oil
60 g (2 oz) butter, melted
400 g (14 oz) button mushrooms, sliced
2 garlic cloves, crushed
¼ teaspoon dried thyme or oregano
300 ml (½ pint) vegetable or chicken stock
3 courgettes, sliced
1 large leek, sliced
2 tablespoons flour
2 x 250 g tub Quark
3 free-range eggs, beaten and seasoned
a little freshly grated nutmeg
40 g (1½ oz) German Emmenthal, grated
sea salt and freshly ground black pepper

1 Heat the oil in a deep saucepan with half the butter, and when hot mix in the mushrooms and garlic. Cook them over a high heat until just softened. Do not let them become watery. Season and stir in the thyme or oregano. Remove from the pan.

2 Add the stock to the pan, bring to the boil then drop in the courgettes and leeks. Simmer for 2–3 minutes until just tender, strain off the stock and reserve.

3 Return the mushrooms to the pan with the vegetables and mix in the flour. When blended stir the stock back in and bring to the boil, stirring until smooth. Simmer for 2 minutes then stir in 3 tablespoons of the Quark.

4 Pour the vegetables into an ovenproof shallow baking dish. Heat the oven to Gas Mark 5/190°C/375°F.

5 Beat the remaining Quark with the egg and seasoning. Pour over the vegetables, scatter over nutmeg and then the grated cheese.

6 Place the dish on a baking sheet and bake for about 30 minutes until the topping is golden brown and bubbling. Allow to stand for 5 minutes before serving. Chunky rye bread and a light beer make good accompaniments.

cabbage or beetroot makes a decorative garnish, as do any of the German vegetable pickles. Finally grind over some coarse black pepper or sprinkle with paprika or chopped fresh herbs. A sprig of fresh dill or flat leaf parsley adds a nice touch.

Here are some suggestions:
• Cooked and sliced Bratwurst sausages with curry-flavoured mayonnaise, blended with Quark and a little milk, on toasted rye bread topped with chopped cucumber.
• Teewurst sausage spread on Pumpernickel breads or cocktail rounds, with a fruit chutney or pickled red cabbage or chopped beetroot.
• Sliced Frankfurters or Bockwurst on light rye bread, spread with sweet German mustard, lettuce and slices of cherry tomatoes or radishes.

Sandwiches
Butterbrot-Variationen

A good sandwich is more than a light snack in Germany. It is a state-of-the-art light meal eaten with a knife and fork. You can create whatever recipe you like choosing from certain basic elements.

First you must have a base of some good fresh bread – these can be sliced Pumpernickel and rye breads sold in packs of 6–8 slices or fresh rye-style breads sold in certain supermarkets. These breads are not only attractive and tasty, but remain moist. Spread with butter or one of the German soft cheeses or cheese spreads. Lay a leaf of lettuce on top or a small bunch of rocket or lamb's lettuce. Add a slice or two of cold sliced meat – salami, ham sausage, Bierwurst, liver sausage – or fish. Vegetarians could use sliced hard-boiled eggs, spears of cooked white asparagus or sautéed mush-rooms. Top with small spoonfuls of ready-prepared salads such as cucumber, herring and potato. Pickled red

Nuremberg sausages

The Nuremberg sausage is the sausage that got smaller and smaller. Legend has it that the 1497 decree reducing its size was so that butchers could pass them through keyholes without breaking Nuremberg's 9 o'clock curfew. But in reality it was the lack of quality ingredients at the time that brought about the incredible shrinking sausage, which won out as the other sausages maintained size but gradually lost quality. Today the Nuremberg sausage is still proof that the best things come in small packages.

**To walk into a German
bakery is to walk
into a food
lovers' paradise**

Breads

Bread is taken very seriously in Germany. High street bakers flourish and varieties abound. What is even more impressive is that German bread tends to be of the healthy wholegrain type, packed with flavour and nutrients. The most popular breads include rye flour either with or without wheat. Rye flour has low levels of gluten and so the texture tends to be denser. Wheat is added to give a lighter texture and a good crust. Seeds and whole grains are popular additions for flavour and texture and, of course, regional variations mean breads come in many shapes and sizes. Darker rye breads have a moist and chewy texture and store for a good length of time without going stale. They are a particularly good way to start the day at breakfast time topped with thinly sliced cheese and ham. At the other end of the texture scale, tasty wheat dough pretzels are slow baked until crisp for light snacks.

FARM BREAD (Landbrot) This is Germany's daily bread – made from wheat with a little light rye flour for a moist texture.

FIVE SEED BREAD (Fünfkornbrot) This bread is made from wheat, rye, barley, oat and maize grains.

THREE SEED BREAD (Mehrkornbrot) Contains rye, wheat and oats. The square shape makes it ideal for sandwiches.

SUNFLOWER SEED BREAD (Sonnenblumenbrot) Baked to a light crunchy texture and mellow flavour.

WHOLEGRAIN RYE BREAD (Katenbrot) 'Katenbrot' means barn-bread. It is eaten with cheese, Quark or cold meats.

WHOLEGRAIN RYE BREAD (Vollkorn) This is typical of the rustic robust bread found on many German tables.

PUMPERNICKEL This rich, dark 100% rye bread is made by a unique method involving time, skill and care.

ROLLS (Semmeln) Light wheat and rye rolls are scored and decorated with poppy seeds, sunflower seeds and sesame seeds.

PRETZELS, ROLLS AND STICKS Crisp and salty pretzel rolls and sticks have been popular in Germany for decades.

PRETZELS Fresh pretzels have a dark, salty crust and delicious chewy bagel-style texture.

SNACKS These salty snacks include some unusual peanut flips. Ideal with drinks.

SNACKS Lower in fat than crisps or peanuts. Try sandwiching knot-shaped pretzels with cream cheese.

Cheese

**Germany produces
every kind of cheese
your cheese board needs**

German cheeses are classified according to their moisture content from firm to easy spreading cream cheeses. The name of the classification will give you a good idea of the texture. Hartkäse are hard or firm cheeses such as Emmentaler and Bergkäse, the mountain cheese. Medium firm cheeses (Schnittkäse)

include Tilsiter and Butterkäse. Soft cheeses (Weichkäse) include the pungent Limburger and popular German bries. Germany also produces many processed cheeses (Schmelzkäse) made from top quality cheeses that have been melted and shaped into logs or processed in rectangular moulds giving them distinctive flavours and shapes. These cheeses are often smoked or have added flavourings such as ham or nuts. Cheeses prefaced with the name Allgäuer originate from certain regions in the Alps in the great cheese-producing region of Bavaria. Cheeses bearing the name Räucherkäse are naturally smoked often over beech wood.

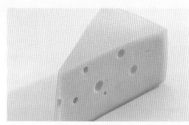

ALLGÄUER BERGKÄSE A firm-textured cheese. An excellent choice for those who like a full flavour.

RED-RINDED SOFT CHEESE The tasty, robust and aromatic rind matches perfectly with the creamy, soft, velvety consistency.

NATURAL SMOKED CHEESE (Räucherkäse) A naturally beechwood-smoked hard cheese, available plain or with chilli flecks.

MINI CHEESE LOGS Soft spreadable processed cheese with orange and hazelnut coating.

WHITE VEINED BRIE Soft, ripened premium cheese with a red rind. A Bavarian speciality.

TILSITER A medium firm cheese with a mid-yellow creamy texture and noticeable tang. Best eaten cold.

SOFT CHEESE (Frischkäse) Excellent on toast or crackers or used as a canapé base on crostini and cocktail Pumpernickels.

UNSALTED BUTTER (Süßrahmbutter) Germany makes some of the best butter in the world. There is also an organic version.

SMOKED CHEESE (Räucherkäse) Blocks or slices of Bavarian processed cheese in plain and smoked ham varieties.

BAVARIAN EMMENTALER A classic hard cheese with a mild, nutty flavour. A good cooking, easy-melt cheese.

CAMEMBERT IN CRISPY CRUMBS (Back-Camembert) A ready-to-cook baby size Camembert cheese with a crumb coating.

BAVARIAN BRIE WITH GREEN PEPPER-CORNS A creamy textured cheese with lightly pickled green peppercorns.

BAVARIAN BLUE BRIE (Blauschimmelbrie) This has a delicate blue-veined creamy centre and velvety mould-ripened skin.

CHEESE SPREAD AND CHEESE SLICES Cheese slices are great for hamburgers. Cheese spread comes in many flavours.

FRESH CHEESE TRIANGLE COATED WITH PAPRIKA This is also available coated with chives or peaches and nuts.

Vegetables

The cooking of tubers, roots and green leafy vegetables reaches the realms of high art in the German kitchen. But the most favoured vegetable by far is the potato. From Kartoffelpuffer to fluffy dumplings stuffed with crunchy croûtons, this is definitely not a boring 'veg' on the side. For secrets with Sauerkraut, turn to page 81 and learn about this highly nutritious and tasty storecupboard treasure.

Above: beetroot, carrots, white asparagus and fresh peas.

Market seller selling potatoes

Light potato dumplings with buttery croûtons

Lockere Kartoffelklöße mit Croûtons

German ingenuity in using the versatility of potatoes is well illustrated with this recipe. Mashed potato is mixed with semolina, flour and eggs then shaped around crisp croûtons to add surprise and texture. This is one of the classic accompaniments to many German main courses. For best results, cook the dough as soon as it is cool enough to handle.
Makes 12 to serve 4–6

1 thick slice white bread
25 g (1 oz) butter
800 g (1 lb 12 oz) potatoes, peeled and halved
60 g (2 oz) plain flour
90 g (3 oz) semolina
1 teaspoon salt
some freshly grated nutmeg
2 medium free-range eggs, beaten
freshly ground black pepper

1 Cut the crusts from the bread then cut into twelve 1.5 cm (¾ inch) squares. Heat the butter in a frying pan and toss in the bread. Fry until golden on all sides then drain on paper towels to crisp up.

2 Meanwhile, boil the potatoes until just tender, about 15 minutes. Drain well, then return to the pan to dry off over a low heat for a minute or two. Now either press the potatoes through a potato ricer or mash until smooth. Cool to room temperature.

3 In a large bowl, mix together the flour, semolina, salt, nutmeg and some pepper. Mix in the potato then gradually work in the beaten egg until you have a firm but just soft dough. Add the egg cautiously towards the end in case you make the mixture too soft.

4 Bring a large pan of salted water to the boil. Using floury hands, scoop up a tablespoon of mixture and shape into a smooth ball. Press a buttery croûton in the centre and reshape. Repeat with all the mixture. Drop the dough balls into the boiling water and turn the heat to medium. Cook uncovered, for about 12–15 minutes. When the balls rise to the surface allow a couple minutes more then remove with a slotted spoon. Don't drain the pan into a colander or you will squash the light texture of the dumplings.

5 Drizzle with melted butter if liked, and serve. In Germany, potato dumplings are sometimes served sprinkled with hot buttery crumbs fried until crisp.

Variation
You could, if you prefer, make larger dumplings filled with several croûtons as shown in the photograph.

Heaven and earth

Himmel und Erde

Potatoes were first known as 'earth apples' in 18th-century Germany. It obviously didn't take long for some clever cook to mix the two ingredients together and produce this unusual mash. Serve it with any main course meat dish. Good with pan-fried liver or pork or veal fillets. Also nice with beef stews and roast venison, goose or duck.
Serves 6

1 kg (2 lb) floury potatoes, peeled
1 kg (2 lb) tart dessert apples, peeled, cored and quartered
a good knob of butter
1 tablespoon rapeseed oil
100 g (3½ oz) Katenspeck, chopped
1 large onion, chopped
sea salt and freshly ground black pepper

1 Boil the potatoes in salted water for about 15 minutes until just tender. Drain then press through a potato ricer or mash well.

2 Meanwhile, cook the apples in about 4 tablespoons of water with a little butter, stirring occasionally until they break down to a purée. Mix into the potato and season well. Set aside and keep warm.

3 Heat the oil in a frying pan and sauté the Katenspeck for about 5–7 minutes until cooked and crispy. Scoop on top of the potato-apple mix. Add the onion to the pan and sauté for 5 minutes until softened and golden.

4 Mix these into the potato and apple, check the seasoning and serve.

Spiced red cabbage

Rotkohl

This is one of Germany's national dishes. You can either buy it ready-made and add some spices of your own, or you can make the version below. Great with roast goose and duck but also popular with venison, game, beef, pork – the list is almost endless. Make it ahead, then reheat for the flavours to mellow.
Serves 4–6

1 medium red cabbage
1 large cooking apple
1 onion, sliced
2 teaspoons soft brown sugar
3 tablespoons wine or apple vinegar
½ teaspoon either ground allspice or cumin or caraway seeds
a good knob of butter
sea salt and freshly ground black pepper

1 Quarter the cabbage, cut out the central core and shred. Quarter, core, peel and chop the apple.

2 Put everything together in a large heavy-based saucepan with about 300 ml (½ pint) water.

3 Bring to the boil, then cover and simmer very gently for about 30 minutes, stirring once or twice. The cabbage should be tender but not soft and the liquid absorbed so the mixture looks glossy. Serve hot. If making ahead, cool and chill. Reheat thoroughly to serve.

Sauerkraut

It's ironic that Germany's national dish in fact originated with the Tartars who lived in what is now China. Sailors took vitamin-C-laden Sauerkraut to sea to prevent scurvy. It is recognised today as a healthy and delicious food. It is eaten hot with pork and fish or cold with salad, and there are many variations. Added ingredients include caraway and juniper, beer and wine, apples, onions, cloves and peppercorns.

Sauerkraut is made from finely shredded white cabbage which is layered with salt in large vats. The vats are then pressurised and fertmentation begins. This produces lactic acid which gives Sauerkraut its unique flavour.

Spiced honey-glazed kohlrabi
Honigglasierten Kohlrabi

Kohlrabi is a turnip that grows large encircling leaves like a cabbage. The stalks of the leaves are attached to the tuber and should be cut off, then the pale green skin peeled. After that, treat it like a turnip, although it has a more delicate flavour. Boil or bake in the oven.
Serves 4

1 large or 2 smaller kohlrabi, peeled
25 g (1 oz) butter
1 tablespoon clear German honey
2 tablespoons orange juice
a good pinch of ground cinnamon
a good pinch of ground allspice
sea salt and freshly ground black pepper

1 Cut the kohlrabi into thick slices then par-boil for 5 minutes in boiling salted water. Drain in a colander, season and preheat the oven to Gas Mark 4/180°C/350°F.

2 Put the remaining ingredients in the same pan and heat until melted and runny.

3 Toss in the blanched kohlrabi then tip into a shallow ovenproof dish. Bake for 20–25 minutes, spooning the glaze over the vegetables as they bake so they take on a delicious honey-brown glaze. Serve hot. Kohlrabi are good with pork and lamb.

Vegetables at market

Baby turnips, carrots and green beans with crunchy Quark topping

Gratin von jungem Gemüse und Quark

A good all-in-one vegetable accompaniment or light main meal vegetarian dish.
Serves 4–6

250 g (9 oz) baby turnips
250 g (9 oz) carrots
250 g (9 oz) whole green beans
a good knob of butter
1 tablespoon chopped fresh chives
1 tablespoon chopped fresh chervil or
    1 teaspoon chopped tarragon
250 g carton Quark
2 tablespoons dried breadcrumbs
2 tablespoons chopped roasted hazelnuts
    or toasted almonds
50 g (1¾ oz) Emmenthal cheese, grated
sea salt and freshly ground black pepper

1 Top and tail the turnips then cut into quarters or large bite-size chunks. Peel the carrots and cut in thick batons. Top and tail the beans and cut in half.

2 Boil the turnips and carrots together in salted water to cover for 5 minutes then stir in the green beans. Return to the boil and cook for another 3–5 minutes, depending on how tender you like your vegetables.

3 Drain well then return the vegetables to the pan. Toss with the butter, herbs, seasoning and finally mix in the Quark. Reheat until piping hot.

4 Transfer to a shallow heatproof dish. Mix the crumbs, nuts and cheese together and scatter over the top of the vegetables.

5 Grill under a medium heat under golden brown and bubbling. Serve immediately.

Fruit juice

Bottles and cartons of fresh fruit juice are popular non-alcoholic drinks throughout Germany and are all characterised by a pure, real fruit flavour. The high quality juices which are exported are made with home-grown apples, cherries and red grapes. Of course, it goes without saying that no artificial additives, colourings or preservatives are used – just pure natural juices.

Beetroot with blue cheese melt

Rote Bete mit Blauschimmelbrie gratiniert

In the UK, beetroot is rarely eaten as a hot vegetable, mostly confined to salad bowls soused in sharp vinegar. But served fresh and hot it is a delightful vegetable and surprisingly versatile. This is a simple and dramatic accompaniment to go with roast lamb or chicken – or great as a quick vegetarian main meal.
Serves 4–6

500 g (1 lb 2 oz) raw beetroot
25 g (1 oz) butter
a good pinch of ground cumin
2 tablespoons chopped fresh chives,
    or 1 salad onion, chopped
100 g (3½ oz) Bavarian blue brie
sea salt and freshly ground black pepper

1 Scrub the beetroot but do not peel. Place in a pan of boiling salted water and simmer for 15–20 minutes until tender when pierced.

2 Drain in a colander and run under cold water to cool sufficiently for you to peel and cut into large bite-size chunks. (Use rubber gloves to protect your hands from staining.)

3 Heat the butter in the same pan and toss in the beetroot with the cumin and seasoning.

4 Reheat until piping hot then sprinkle over the chives or onions. Tip into a heatproof dish.

5 De-rind the blue cheese if necessary and cut either into slivers or cubes. Arrange on top of the beets and place under a hot grill to just melt. Serve immediately.

84

White asparagus with veal escalope and potato

A feast for the senses

Asparagus, apples and plums

Isn't it refreshing to find a fresh food that is truly seasonal? Well, from mid April to the end of June, Euro gourmets indulge in many feasts of the senses with plump juicy German white asparagus. Special asparagus menus appear in many restaurants and food shops proudly display towering bundles of luscious creamy velvety stems.

When you buy a bundle of white asparagus, the stems will be firm, crisp and plump, and have a characteristic velvety sheen. The tips should be intact and firm, sometimes showing a slight purple tinge. If you

don't intend cooking them straightaway, wrap in a damp tea towel and store in the base of the fridge.

Peel almost the whole stem with a swivel vegetable peeler from the tip downwards. Chop off any woody ends. If possible use a tall asparagus steamer, but otherwise a large covered sauté or frying pan will do. Bring a pan of water to the boil and add a teaspoon each of salt, sugar and butter. Cover and simmer for about 10 minutes. Drain well, taking care not to damage the delicate tips. Drizzle with melted butter or oil and vinegar dressing.

Germany is a great fruit-growing country with a long history of producing top-quality orchard fruits, such as apples and plums. Both feature in many traditional recipes as cakes, jellies and jams, and in savoury dishes too.

The most popular German apples you will find on sale in the UK are Cox's, Braeburn, Rubinette and the top chefs' favourite, the Jonagold which has a delightful aromatic sweet-sour fruity balance. It is one of the best apples for baking or for making pies and Tarte Tatin.

Plums proliferate in the state of Baden; the season stretches from July to September. Baden plums are ideal for cooking or eating fresh. They have a firm, fruity flesh and a sweet/sharp juicy flavour. They make lovely summer fruit soups and are a must for plum jam. If poached lightly in cinnamon-flavoured sugar syrup, they make a delicious topping for cheesecake. Or drain them and wrap in layers of Strudel pastry with dollops of sweetened Quark.

(above) Basket of GERMAN APPLES, (left) BADEN PLUMS (Zwetschen)

Honeys and jams

If you ever have the opportunity to go shopping in Germany be prepared to be bowled over by the incredible selection of wild honeys and full fruity jams, many in shops specially dedicated to these preserves. Fragrant flowers and aromatic plants give differing characteristics to the honeys, from wild herb and wildflower to dandelion and pine-scented. Jams include not only cultivated fruits but wild berries such as the delightful elderberry.

Cakes and Desserts

It will come as no surprise, that as the land of the best cheesecakes in the world, Germany has many other ways with delicious desserts. Germany's most versatile dairy ingredient, Quark, features in many recipes. It bakes and cooks without splitting or curdling, it comes in very low-fat varieties and yet it still tastes satisfyingly creamy. There are some other sweet surprises in this chapter: you'll discover that dark and nutty Pumpernickel is very successful in sweet dishes, poppy seeds can be used for more than just a sprinkle on top and we've even included a British-style bread and butter pudding with rich, almond Stollen.

Above: ice cream and fruit.

Gingerbread hearts (Lebkuchenherzen) bearing the legend, 'I love you'. These come in every colour and with every sort of sentimental message

Chocolate and cherry torte
Schokoladen-Kirsch-Torte

Make a light textured dark chocolate cake in the shape of a sponge flan base. Top with whipped cream and Quark and either fresh raspberries or cherries in syrup with a little thickened juice from the fruits.
Serves 6–8

100 g (3½ oz) caster sugar
1 sachet vanilla sugar or ½ teaspoon
    vanilla essence
4 free-range eggs
100 g (3½ oz) plain flour
½ teaspoon baking powder
25 g (1 oz) cocoa powder
100 g (3½ oz) ground hazelnuts or
    almonds
100 g (3½ oz) grated chocolate
680 g jar cherries in syrup
1 teaspoon cornflour or potato starch
200 ml (7 fl oz) double cream
half 250 g tub Quark
1 tablespoon caster sugar, or to taste

1 Grease a 28 cm (11-inch) sponge flan tin and dust lightly with a little flour. Heat the oven to Gas Mark 4/180°C/350°F.

2 Whisk the sugar, vanilla sugar or essence with the eggs until thick and creamy when the mixture leaves a trail when the beaters are lifted up. This is best done with an electric whisk.

3 Sift the flour, baking powder and cocoa powder together. Fold into the mixture then add the nuts and grated chocolate.

4 Spoon into the tin, level the top and bake for about 30 minutes until firm and cooked. Cool for 5 minutes in the tin, then turn out and cool completely.

5 Drain the cherries, reserving 100 ml of the juice. (Use the rest in a jelly or drink if you don't want to waste it.) Slake the cornflour or potato starch with a tablespoon of the juice.

6 Heat the saved juice until boiling. Mix a little hot liquid with the slaked starch and then pour all of it into the pan and simmer until thickened. Cool slightly then mix with the fruits and cool completely until glossy.

7 Whip the cream until it forms soft peaks and fold in the Quark and a tablespoon of caster sugar. Spoon on top of the flan case. Drizzle over the glossy fruits. Cool until set then serve cut in wedges.

Festivals

There is a multitude of local festivals throughout Germany each year, including the Ratcatcher's Parade in Hamelin, the Dürkheim Sausage Festival and the many wine festivals around the Rhine and Mosel areas. The most celebrated of these is the Munich Oktoberfest, held unaccountably in September each year, for two weeks of indulgence in beer. More popular even than this is Carnival; the history of this feast day stretches back to ancient civilisations and is an intriguing mixture of pagan and Christian as townsfolk let off steam and drink and dance for three whole days.

Marinated fruits in rum
Rumtopf

This is not a quick recipe, because you have to start it several weeks before you intend serving it, but it is easy. To make it in the classic manner you are advised to buy a large stoneware 'Rumtopf' jar which is slightly porous and best stored in a cool dark place such as an old-fashioned larder. As few of us have larders then a garden shed or base of a fridge will have to do. There are no exact recipes for making Rumtopf, because the idea is that you add seasonal fruits, sugar and rum in proportion to each other as summer leads into autumn. Then at Christmas time (or thereabouts) find a good excuse for a party and enjoy the fruits of your labours – literally. Ice cream or sweetened Quark are good accompaniments, or use the fruits as the base of a trifle layered with sponge finger biscuits and coffee-flavoured whipped cream. However, you don't have to use the Rumtopf all at once; spoon into it as the mood takes you.

To start the Rumtopf:
1 kilo soft fruits – stoned cherries, plums, raspberries, blackberries, straw-berries, sliced peaches, red, white and blackcurrants, billberries
360 g (12 oz) caster sugar
1 litre strong dark rum
To add to the Rumtopf:
seasonal fruits in the proportion of 500 g (1 lb 2 oz) for every 180 g (6 oz) sugar
extra dark rum as required

1 Pick over the fruit and make sure none of it is damaged or dirty. You need to ensure the fruits do not go mouldy as they mature. Mix the fruits and sugar in a large bowl overnight until the juices start to run.

2 Mix in the rum and spoon into a special Rumtopf jar or tall glass preserving jar. Make sure the fruits are submerged beneath the liquid: cover with a 'cartouche' (a sheet of wet greaseproof paper scrunched up) and one or two saucers to weigh the fruits down. Cover with a lid.

3 As the summer progresses, add more fruits and sugar in the proportions given above, stirring the contents gently to mix. Seal again with a clean cartouche and the lid. You can add more rum if liked after about 4 weeks. However, it is not essential although it does give it a lively kick.

Lemon, marzipan and poppy seed mousses

Zitronencreme mit Marzipan und Mohn

Poppy seeds appear in many German dessert and cake recipes. Often they are ground to a dry purée, which can be done in a small electric grinder – see Almond and Poppy Biscuit Cups (page 98). Marzipan can be bought in blocks and coarsely grated to fold into the mousse mixture. This makes a lovely summer dessert to serve with fresh raspberries and blueberries. Makes 6–8

50 g (1¾ oz) poppy seeds
4 large free-range eggs (size 1–2),
    separated
120 g (4 oz) caster sugar
4 tablespoons water
grated zest and juice of 2 lemons
1 sachet gelatine crystals
284 ml carton double cream, lightly
    whipped
75 g marzipan, chilled and chopped finely

1 Grind the poppy seeds in a small electric mill until fine then set aside.

2 Put the egg yolks, sugar, water, lemon zest and juice into a large bowl. Set over a saucepan of simmering water and, using an electric hand-held whisk, beat until pale yellow, thick and foamy. The foam should be thick enough to leave a trail when lifted up.

3 Remove the bowl from the pan and continue whisking for about 3 minutes to cool down.

4 Put 2 tablespoons of cold water into a cup and sprinkle over the gelatine. Let the gelatine soak into the water to a 'sponge' and then dissolve either in a microwave on defrost power for about 2 minutes or place the cup in a small pan of simmering water.

5 Beat the gelatine into the whisked mixture and leave until room temperature. Whisk the cream until it makes soft peaks then fold into the mixture along with the poppy seeds and grated marzipan.

6 When the mixture is on the point of setting, whisk the egg whites with a good pinch of salt until they make soft peaks. Beat two spoons of this into the mixture to loosen, then fold the rest in using a large metal spoon. Divide the soufflé between 6 to 8 elegant sundae glasses. Chill until firm.

7 Decorate as you wish. Whirls of piped whipped cream would be nice topped with a small ratafia or small, thin slices of fresh lemon, or grated lemon zest.

Tree cakes

The traditional and original German tree cakes or Baumkuchen are laboriously produced by baking over an open fire. Each thin ring is cooked individually on a wooden roller and then another layer is added to slowly form the cake. The cooled cake is then glazed with chocolate or icing. Traditionally the whole cake is then brought to the table before being admired, thinly sliced and enjoyed. The cake was created in 1820. According to the legend, Luise, a musician's daughter, was working as a pastry chef in the town of Salzwedel. She came across the recipe in one of her grandfather's notebooks, written during his travels in France.

Baked Jonagold apples with marzipan and cranberry

Jonagold-Bratäpfel mit Marzipan und Moosbeeren

Germany's Jonagold apples are perfect bakers. The flesh becomes creamy and smooth and the flavour intense, while the attractive skin keeps its colour.
Serves 4

4 large German Jonagold apples
3 tablespoons redcurrant jelly
75 g (2¾ oz) fresh or frozen cranberries, thawed
100 g pack marzipan, chopped
To serve:
125 g (4½ oz) Quark
142 ml carton whipping cream
1 tablespoon caster sugar
½ teaspoon ground cinnamon

1 Using an apple corer, remove the core from each apple. Insert the corer three or four times more to make a wider hole. Using the tip of a small sharp knife, score round the middle of each apple, to help the apples keep their shape.

2 Heat the oven to Gas Mark 3/170°C/320°F. Lightly warm the redcurrant jelly in a small pan until runny and heat the cranberries for a minute or two in it. Don't cook them.

3 Cool the mixture for a few minutes – you'll find it becomes firm. Stand the apples upright in a small baking dish.

4 Press a little marzipan into the hollow of each apple. Spoon over some cranberry mixture. Add more marzipan, then more cranberry and so on, finishing by glazing the top of each apple with some cranberry mixture. Repeat with the other apples.

5 Bake for 45–50 minutes, basting each apple with the juices about three times. Pierce the centres to check when they are cooked, but don't let the apples collapse. They should have lightly wrinkled skins with just-softened flesh.

6 Remove and cool, spooning the glaze over once or twice. Mix the Quark, cream, sugar and cinnamon and serve alongside the apples.

Cherry, Quark and Pumpernickel trifle

Sauerkirschdessert mit Pumpernickel

This quick dessert is ideal if you want to cause a stir at a dinner party. Make stunning layers in a chic plain glass serving bowl. Or for individual servings, use elegant wine glasses.
Serves 6

2 x 250 g tubs Quark
150 ml (¼ pint) milk
1 sachet vanilla sugar or 1 teaspoon
    vanilla essence
3 tablespoons caster sugar
2 slices Pumpernickel
50 g (1¾ oz) dark chocolate or 100 g
    (3½ oz) ratafia biscuits
680 g jar German cherries in juice

1 Beat together the Quark, milk, vanilla sugar or essence plus the caster sugar until smooth.

2 Whizz the Pumpernickel in a food processor to fine crumbs. Finely grate the chocolate or crush the ratafias. Mix with the Pumpernickel crumbs.

3 Drain the cherries well. Now make layers in a large glass dish or 6 wine glasses. Put cherries at the base and spoon on some Quark. Scatter over the Pumpernickel. Repeat the layers saving a few cherries and crumbs for the top. Finish with a Quark layer then plop the last few cherries randomly on top and sprinkle lightly with crumbs for an attractive finish. Chill overnight and serve.

Passion fruit and Quark soufflés
Quark Soufflés

I have to thank Anton Edelmann, Executive Chef of the Savoy, for the inspiration for this recipe. Using Quark in a baked soufflé base makes a wonderfully light dessert. Ensure your diners are waiting for these at the table as they sink when they cool.
Makes 8

250 g tub Quark
2 free-range egg yolks
grated zest and juice of 1 large orange
4 ripe passion fruits
2 tablespoons cornflour
6 tablespoons icing sugar
a little softened butter and caster sugar,
**   for lining the ramekins**
3 free-range egg whites
a good pinch of sea salt

1 Beat the Quark, yolks, orange zest and juice until smooth. Halve the passion fruits and scoop the flesh into a sieve set over a bowl.

Rub the juice and pulp through. Stir this into the Quark mix with the cornflour and half the sugar.

2 Prepare eight medium-size ramekins. Brush the sides and base with melted butter then shake sugar inside so it coats the ramekins. Tap out any excess. Place these in a roasting tin. Heat the oven to Gas Mark 5/190°C/375°F.

3 Whisk the egg whites with the pinch of salt to make soft peaks. Whisk in the remaining sugar. You should have a firm, stiff foam.

4 Fold into the Quark mixture then divide between the ramekins, levelling the tops with the back of a teaspoon. Pour boiling water into the roasting tin to come halfway up the sides of the ramekins. Carefully place in the oven and bake for about 20 minutes or so, until risen. With a fish slice quickly lift the ramekins out, wipe dry, and place on serving plates. Serve immediately.

Homemade apple and cherry Strudel
Hausgemachter Apfel-Kirschstrudel

Strudel pastry is a soft dough that is gently pulled by hand until it is so thin you can see through it. It is actually not difficult to make. In fact it can be quite therapeutic letting the soft dough drape over your hands as you work it thinner and thinner. You may well get a few tears in the pastry but these can easily be rolled in, so don't worry. A homely look is more inviting, as is a liberal dusting of icing sugar to cover up any little imperfections. Serve with lightly sweetened whipped cream.
Serves 8

250 g (9 oz) plain flour + extra for rolling
a good pinch of salt
1 free-range egg, beaten
½ teaspoon white wine vinegar
100 g (3½ oz) butter, melted and cooled
4–5 tablespoons water
icing sugar to dust
For the filling:
400 g (14 oz) tart apples
200 g (7 oz) fresh cherries
3–4 tablespoons chopped roasted hazel
**   nuts or toasted flaked almonds**

3–4 tablespoons caster sugar
½ teaspoon cinnamon
5 tablespoons semolina

1 Sift the flour and salt into an electric mixer then mix in the egg, vinegar, half the melted butter and 4 tablespoons of water until you have a soft, shiny dough. You may need the last tablespoon of water depending on the flour. Knead to a smooth ball then leave to rest for 20 minutes under an upturned bowl.

2 Prepare the filling while you wait. Peel and slice the apples, stone and halve the cherries. Mix them with the hazelnuts or almonds, sugar and cinnamon. Set aside. Preheat the oven to Gas Mark 4/180°C/350°F.

3 Spread a clean old tablecloth out on a work-top or table – preferably one you can get round easily. Sprinkle with flour. First roll out the dough to a large rectangle as far as you can. When it becomes too thin to roll, transfer the task to your hands.

4 Slide your hands under the dough palms facing downwards. Working from the centre outwards and with your hands forming a half 'fist' so your knuckles are prominent, gently work the dough until you can see the pattern of the cloth underneath. Try hard not to tear the dough as you stretch it. But if you do, it is not the end of the world.

5 When you have stretched the dough to a rectangle about 75 cm (29 inches) square, trim the thicker edges with scissors.

6 Brush all over with half the remaining butter and sprinkle over the semolina.

7 Scatter the filling over the top two thirds of the stretched dough. Fold in the top edge and sides, then using the cloth lift it up to start the rolling, letting the filling and dough fall over and over until the end.

8 When you get near the end, position a large lightly greased baking sheet so that the roll can be manoeuvred onto it. You may have to push it a bit. Form the roll into a horseshoe shape if necessary and brush over the last of the butter.

9 Bake for 35–40 minutes until the pastry is golden brown and crisp. Remove, wait for 10 minutes then loosen the base with a palette knife and allow the roll to slide onto a wire cooling tray. Cool for another 20–30 minutes then dust liberally with icing sugar. Cut into diagonal slices to serve.

Pumpernickel ice cream

Vanilleeis mit Pumpernickel

This is not so unlikely as may at first appear and is quite similar to British brown bread ice cream. The tangy rich Pumpernickel crumbs give a delicious flavour to a vanilla flavoured custard. Serve with poached plums in syrup or Summer Fruit Pudding (right). This is a good ice cream to have in your freezer for impromptu entertaining. An ice-cream machine helps give you a smooth, creamy texture.
Serves 8

150 g (5 oz) Pumpernickel
500 ml (18 fl oz) milk
500 ml (18 fl oz) double cream
3 medium free-range eggs
4 free-range egg yolks
150 g (5 oz) caster sugar
1 sachet vanilla sugar or 1 teaspoon
    vanilla essence

1 Grind the Pumpernickel to fine crumbs in a food processor.

2 Heat the milk and cream in a large non-stick saucepan until on the point of boiling. Meanwhile, whisk the eggs, egg yolks and sugar (and vanilla sugar or essence) until thick and creamy in a large bowl, placed on a damp cloth to hold it steady.

3 When the creamy milk starts to rise pour half of it slowly on the eggs and sugar, whisking briskly. Reheat the remaining milk until it rises again and whisk into the mixture.

4 Strain back into the saucepan, and over a very low heat, stir with a wooden spoon until it thickens a little more and you can draw a line across with the back of the spoon. Immediately remove from the heat and pour back into the bowl to cool.

5 When cool, add the Pumpernickel. Churn in an ice-cream machine until smooth and creamy, then scoop into a freezer container to store in the freezer. If you don't have an ice-cream machine, pour into a freezer container and freeze until slushy. Then remove and beat with a whisk to break up the ice crystals and freeze again. Repeat the whisking and freezing twice.

6 Store the ice cream for up to one month. To serve, allow to soften for 10–15 minutes until soft enough to scoop or spoon.

First day at school

Most Germans remember their first day at school, carrying a paper cone filled with sweets, a 19th century trick to make education (and separation from parents) more palatable. Originally it would have been fruit or sweet pretzels, but the brightly coloured candy has won out in most parts, with the ad men making their mark; outsize ready-made cones can even contain t-shirts and CDs to promote the latest cinema releases for the under-7s. Suggestions by dentists that they should also contain a toothbrush sadly never caught on!

Summer fruit pudding

Rote Grütze

This recipe is Germany's answer to our summer pudding – a wonderful selection of the best of red summer berries, to be served either lightly thickened with a little cornflour (as in this recipe) or set as a jelly. Serve in dainty glass dishes with sweetened Quark flavoured with a touch of vanilla.

Serves 6

1 kilo (2 lb 4 oz) selection of summer berries – strawberries, raspberries, redcurrants, blueberries, stoned cherries
180 g (6 oz) caster sugar
grated zest of 1 orange or 1 lemon
3 tablespoons arrowroot or cornflour

1 Prepare the berries. Hull the strawberries and if necessary cut in half. Strip the redcurrants from the stalks with a fork. Mix with the other fruits of your choice in a bowl with the sugar and grated zest.

2 Cover. Leave for at least 6–8 hours in the fridge to steep until the juices run out. Strain into a small saucepan. Slake the arrowroot or cornflour with 3 tablespoons water. Bring the juices to the boil then stir briskly into the slaked starch.

3 Return to the pan and simmer, stirring, until thickened. Mix into the fruits then divide between 6–8 sundae glasses. Chill until ready to serve.

Almond and poppy seed biscuit cups

Biskuitschalen mit Mohn

Shape the thin mixture over an orange as it cools to make biscuit cups, or make small flat shapes for flat biscuits. Be warned, these are very moreish.

Makes about 12 cups or 24 biscuits

4 free-range egg whites
50 g (1¾ oz) caster sugar
2 tablespoons plain flour
225 g (8 oz) ground almonds
25 g (1 oz) ground poppy seeds
1 tablespoon almond oil

1 Lightly whisk the egg whites then beat in the remaining ingredients to a smooth thick batter.

2 Heat the oven to Gas Mark 4/180°C/350°F. Line a baking sheet with non-stick baking parchment or silicone baking sheeting. For cups, spread dessertspoonfuls of mixture on the sheet, spreading with a wet palette knife to rounds approximately 15 cm (6 inches). For biscuits, drop teaspoonfuls on the sheeting. Allow room for these to spread so it is best to bake them in batches. The batter will not spoil.

3 Bake for about 7 minutes until the edges turn golden brown. Cool for half a minute or so on the tray before lifting off with a palette knife onto a wire tray (for flat biscuits) or over an orange for cups, pressing down gently with your fingers wrapped in a tea towel. Repeat as many times as necessary.

4 Store in an airtight container until required. Serve scoops of Quark and lemon water ice in the cups if liked.

Cook's note

To grind poppy seeds, simply whizz them through an electric coffee or spice mill. Make sure it is thoroughly clean before you add the seeds.

Quark and lemon water ice

Zitronensorbet mit Quark

Use Quark to make a refreshingly clean-tasting water ice. Serve it in shavings layered up in wine glasses. Or serve in scoops in crisp almond and poppy seed biscuit cups.

Serves 8–10

500 ml (18 fl oz) water
250 g (9 oz) sugar
4 black peppercorns
grated zest and juice of 2 lemons
2 x 250 g tubs Quark

1 Dissolve the water and sugar together over a low heat, then add the peppercorns and lemon zest. Boil for 2 minutes then cool and chill overnight. Scoop out the peppercorns and discard.

2 Beat the syrup and lemon juice gradually into the Quark until smooth then either churn in an ice-cream machine until slushy or pour into a shallow freezerproof plastic container and freeze until slushy.

3 Beat the mixture with a whisk and return to the freezer. Repeat two or three times, beating and refreezing the mixture. This helps give it a creamy texture. If churning in a machine, freeze in a rigid container after it turns slushy.

4 Store for up to a month. To serve, soften at room temperature for 15 minutes or so until soft enough to scrape or scoop.

Stollen bread and butter pudding
Süßer Stollenauflauf

Christmas market

A dessert created in the best interests of Anglo-German understanding combining two much loved national favourites! It is wickedly good. Use any Stollen, but the Edel-Marzipan filled one is particularly delicious.

Serves 6–8

500 g Stollen
50 g (1¾ oz) butter, softened for
   spreading
about 100 g (3½ oz) canned cherries in
   syrup, drained (optional)
some demerara sugar to sprinkle
For the custard:
2 medium free-range eggs + 2 egg yolks
284 ml carton double cream
400 ml (14 fl oz) milk
3–4 tablespoons caster sugar
a few drops of almond essence

1 Slice the Stollen thinly and spread one side with butter. Stack in slightly angled layers in a large lightly buttered ovenproof dish. Scatter cherries in between, if used.

2 Beat the eggs and yolks with the cream, milk, caster sugar and essence. Slowly pour over the Stollen slices, pressing them down into the liquid so they are well soaked. Set aside for a good hour to allow the custard to be absorbed.

3 Meanwhile, heat the oven to Gas Mark 4/ 180°C/350°F. Place the dish in a roasting pan and when ready to bake pour in boiling water to come halfway up the dish sides.

4 Carefully place in the oven and bake for about 35 minutes until the top is light golden brown and crisp. Cool for 10–15 minutes before serving, sprinkled with demerara sugar.

Gingerbread house

Christmas baking includes a number of spicy cakes (Lebkuchen) and crisp biscuits. These are often adorned with white and coloured piped sugar decorations. Central to the festivities is the edible Hexenhaus or Gingerbread House, also called Hansel and Gretel's house after the well-known fairy tale. This is made from flat panels of honey and ginger cake fixed together with dabs of icing. Windows, doors, chimneys, even fences are fashioned from cake. Children (of all ages!) decorate them with little biscuits, nuts, gaily coloured sweets and a dusting of icing sugar for snow.

You can now buy a kit version of a Hexenhaus containing everything you need.

Baked German cheesecake

Deutscher Käsekuchen

This is proper cheesecake! Use Quark and cream for the best melt-in-the mouth texture. As a variation add some sultanas to the cheese mixture. Make this the day before you intend to serve it so it can chill and firm. It is best made in a traditional springform cake tin with a removable base.

Serves 6–8

25 cm (10-inch) sponge flan base
2 x 250 g tub Quark
284 ml carton soured cream
284 ml carton double cream
200 g (7 oz) caster sugar
3 large free-range eggs, beaten
juice of 1 lemon
2 sachets vanilla sugar or 2 teaspoons
    vanilla essence
sultanas (optional)
sifted icing sugar, to serve

1 Heat the oven to Gas Mark 3/170°C/320°F. Lightly grease the sides of a 23 cm (9-inch) springform cake tin. Using the base as a template cut out the sponge flan to fit inside the tin.

Line the base first with a disc of baking parchment then press the cut sponge round down on the base of the tin. Make sure it is a snug fit so the liquid mixture doesn't seep out during baking.

2 Beat together the Quark, two creams, sugar, eggs, lemon and vanilla sugar or essence to a smooth cream in a food processor or by hand in a large bowl. (If sultanas are to be used, add two good handfuls at this stage.)

3 Pour on top of the sponge flan base and bake for about 40 minutes until the top is golden brown. Turn off the oven and leave the cake inside to cool for another hour to prevent the surface cracking.

4 Chill the cake in the fridge overnight until very firm, then run a table knife inside the rim of the tin to loosen and remove the cake. Slide a palette knife under the base and slip the cake onto a flat cake platter. Dust the top with sifted icing sugar and serve.

No-bake cheesecake with exotic fruit topping

Käsekuchen mit exotischen Früchten

Here is a simple version of a chilled cheese-cake using Quark and a crushed biscuit base. There are some delicious German biscuits on sale in the UK. If you use a chocolate-covered variety, chill them first and then crush them finely in a food processor to give you a chunky chocolate base. For the topping, use sliced or crushed exotic fruits. As great travellers, Germans have developed a keen taste for exotic fruits and many outdoor markets and food halls boast fabulous displays of fruits from all over the world. Choose whatever you fancy for the top, except kiwis and pineapple, as the juice of these fruits dissolves gelatine. Or you might like to try using fresh raspberries or sliced strawberries with blueberries.

Serves 6

125 g (4 oz) German biscuits
25 g (1 oz) butter
1 tablespoon golden syrup
For the filling:
250 g tub Quark
grated zest of 1 lemon
juice of 2 lemons
5 tablespoons caster sugar
1 sachet vanilla sugar or ½ teaspoon
   vanilla essence
1 sachet gelatine crystals
420 ml carton double cream
200 g (7 oz) of mixed prepared exotic
   fruits, e.g. sliced mango or paw paw,
   or stoned lychees, or thinly sliced
   star fruit etc.

1 If using chocolate biscuits, chill them well first. Crush the biscuits in a food processor. Melt the butter with the syrup and mix into the crushed biscuits and press down well inside a 20 cm (8-inch) flan tin with a removable base. It is best to use a tin that is at least 4 cm (1½ inches) deep for the filling, and to be on the safe side, line the base with a disc of baking parchment. Chill the base while you make the filling.

2 For the filling, wipe out the food processor and whizz the Quark, lemon zest, juice, sugar and vanilla sugar or essence until smooth.

3 Sprinkle the gelatine on about 2 tablespoons of cold water in a cup and leave to 'sponge', then melt in a microwave for 30 seconds or until dissolved. Alternatively, place the cup in a small pan of boiling water and stir once or twice until melted.

4 Beat some of the Quark mixture into the gelatine then scrape it all back into the Quark mix and chill for about 10 minutes or so until it begins to set.

5 Immediately whisk the cream until it makes soft peaks, and fold into the Quark mix. Pour on top of the biscuit base and return to the fridge to chill until firm.

6 When ready to serve, run a table knife round the outside of the set cake and push up and out. Slide a palette knife under the base and place on a flat serving dish. Spoon on your preferred exotic fruit topping and serve cut in wedges.

Baden plum cake
Badischer Zwetschenkuchen

Some of Germany's best plums come from around Baden in the south-west of the country. Sweet, quartered plums are lightly pressed into a sweet, rich yeast dough and baked, then served topped with flaked almonds and lemon sugar.
Serves 6–8

200 g (7 oz) plain flour, sifted with a pinch of salt
1 sachet dried fast-action yeast
40 g (1½ oz) butter, at room temperature
5 tablespoons caster sugar
1 small free-range egg, beaten
100 ml (3½ fl oz) milk, lukewarm
about 750 g (1¾ lb) plums, stoned and quartered
25 g (1 oz) flaked almonds
grated zest of 1 lemon

1 Mix the flour with the yeast, rub in the butter then mix in 3 tablespoons of the sugar. Make a well in the centre then beat in the egg and milk until you have a soft, smooth dough. Mix well in the bowl and knead for about 4 minutes.

2 Grease a 25 cm (10-inch) shallow, round springform cake tin. Roll or pat out the dough to fit the tin. Dip your fingers in flour if the dough sticks. Press it in lightly, taking it right to the edge. Cover and leave to rise until doubled in size, about ½ to 1 hour.

3 Arrange the plum quarters skin-side-down in circles on top. Sprinkle over the remaining sugar.

4 Heat the oven to Gas Mark 4/180°C/350°F and bake the cake for about 35–40 minutes until it is risen and the plums are soft.

5 Cool in the tin and scatter over the almonds and lemon zest. Remove from the tin and cool completely on a wire rack.

Apple, lemon and Kirsch Streusel cake
Apfelstreusel-Kuchen mit Kirschwasser

Streusel is a soft crumbly topping German cooks like to sprinkle on top of cakes before baking. It gives a delicious sweet buttery flavour. Serve this cake in warm wedges with softly whipped cream, which could be spiked with a little more Kirsch.
Serves 6–8

500 g (1 lb 2 oz) German apples, e.g. Jonagold or Rubinette
3 tablespoons Black Forest Kirsch
grated zest of 1 lemon
250 g (9 oz) plain flour
3 teaspoons baking powder

a good pinch of salt
125 g (4½ oz) butter, softened
150 g (5½ oz) caster sugar
1 sachet vanilla sugar or ½ teaspoon
   vanilla essence
2 free-range eggs
2 tablespoons milk
For the topping:
25 g (1 oz) chilled butter
50 g (1¾ oz) plain flour
25 g (1 oz) demerara sugar
1 tablespoon chopped roasted hazelnuts
2 teaspoons grated lemon zest
a good pinch of ground cinnamon

1 Toss the apples in the Kirsch and lemon zest and leave to macerate for ½ hour. Sift the flour with the baking powder and salt.

2 Grease and line a 20 cm (8-inch) deep round cake tin, ideally loose-bottomed or springform. Heat the oven to Gas Mark 3/170°C/320°F.

3 Beat the butter and sugar with the vanilla sugar or essence until creamy and fluffy then mix in the eggs. Fold in the flour and finally the milk. Stir in the apples when they have absorbed the flavour of the Kirsch and zest.

4 Make the topping by rubbing the chilled butter into the flour until it resembles fine breadcrumbs. Add the remaining ingredients.

5 Spoon the cake mix into the prepared tin, level off the top and sprinkle over the topping. Bake for 1 to 1¼ hours until risen and golden brown. Cool for 10 minutes then turn out onto a wire rack to cool. Serve freshly baked and cut in wedges with dollops of whipped sweetened cream, flavoured with another tablespoon or two of Kirsch!

Quark

Quark has been part of the German culinary heritage for centuries

and yogurt

In the Alps at the end of the summer cows are brought down from the high mountain pastures where they have grazed in the summer. The cows wear a flower head dress and a large bell.

Germany is a country of rich dairy pastures, from the north of the country right down to the alpine region of Bavaria. Two top-quality fresh cultured products, widely available in the UK are Quark (a skimmed milk soft cheese) and yogurt.

Quark accounts for over half the cheese sold in Germany. Traditionally, it was made by draining small amounts of warm, soured milk in cotton sacks overnight. This produced curds and whey leaving a lightly tangy, delicious and very useful fresh young cheese. Unlike many other dairy ingredients, Quark does not separate when heated

YOGURT WITH CHOCOLATE SHAVINGS

YOGURT WITH HAZELNUTS

YOGURT WITH APPLE STRUDEL

YOGURT WITH BLOOD ORANGE

QUARK RICE WITH STRAWBERRY

QUARK MOUSSE DESSERT

QUARK

SAVOURY QUARK

YOGURT WITH MUESLI

and so can be used with confidence in cooking and baking. The high lactic acid content also preserves the cheese and gives it a longer shelf life.

Quark is high in first-class proteins and vitamins, and is a good source of calcium. Quark is sold in three varieties depending on the butterfat content. 1% butterfat is the most commonly available in the UK. This has just 75 calories per 100 g, making it perfect for a low-fat diet. Next is a 5% butterfat content, but even the richest Quark is only 10-12%

butterfat, that is less than single cream. Organic Quark at 10% fat is widely available from good health food stores and is a wonderful treat for breakfast or as a topping for hot dishes. Unlike cottage cheese Quark has a smooth velvety texture because it is not heated before the curds and whey are drained. Even the very low-fat variety is not at all grainy and can be spread on toast or bread, used in canapés or spooned into baked potatoes straight from the tub. Wherever you want to add a dairy

cream taste for very little fat, add a good spoonful or two of creamy Quark. It is also the soft cheese to use for traditional cheesecakes.

German yogurt has an excellent reputation in the UK for top quality and smoothness and German companies have pioneered many new and exciting varieties. Ranging from wholemilk to very low fat and milder bio styles, these include a delectable range of popular and exotic fruit and nut flavours, even apple Strudel and Schnaps with chocolate shavings.

**Baking is something of an art form
in Germany and every town boasts
a traditional bakers and confectioners**

Biscuits,
cakes and confectionery

Many German cakes and biscuits have their origins in a rich and colourful history going back many centuries. Biscuits, cakes and sweet rich yeast breads are crafted into complex patterns and shapes, often associated with ancient symbolic meanings.

Two famous German cakes which are now exported to many countries in the world are Stollen and Lebkuchen. They are especially popular around Christmas time. In fact, many British consumers now enjoy these cakes more than the heavier British Christmas pudding and Christmas cake. Rich, sweet, yeast Stollens dusted with icing sugar are said to represent the infant Christ wrapped in swaddling clothes. Inside are 'gifts' of fruits, nuts and brightly coloured candied delicacies. The best known Stollen comes from Dresden, but many regions have their own delicious variations.

Honey-sweet, richly spiced ginger Lebkuchen can be traced back to the early days of the European spice trade when sugar was an expensive luxury and honey the common sweetener. Some Lebkuchen are coated with chocolate and sold in many shapes and sizes. Beautifully packaged, large, flat, sugar-glazed Lebkuchen 'buns' are popular Christmas gifts.

Marzipan (the early European 'March pane' or bread of March used to celebrate the Eastertide festivities) is governed by strict

BAUMKUCHEN An unusual cake
from Salzwedel in East Germany

MARZIPAN ANIMALS

DOMINOSTEINE and PRINTEN

LEBKUCHEN

ELISEN LEBKUCHEN on RICE PAPER

CHOCOLATE

MARZIPAN STOLLEN and BUTTER STOLLEN

MARBLE CAKE and HAZELNUT CAKE

MARZIPAN LOAVES

ASSORTED CHOCOLATES

MOZART KUGELN

SWEET BISCUITS

SWEET BISCUITS

food laws ensuring a blend of two parts ground almonds to one part sugar. Marzipan bearing the name Edelmarzipan must have a minimum of 70% unadulterated marzipan. Also, rose water is the only flavouring permitted – although many shapes are then dusted with flavoured icing sugars.

From the nineteenth century onwards, chocolate production bene-fitted from German technology and strict purity laws to become an affordable luxury for everyone. Today,

strict percentages of cocoa mass, cocoa butter, milk, cream and sugar must be adhered to in all chocolate production. German chocolate is generally not as high in sugar as British chocolate, contains no vege-table fat and gives a good clean bite.

In the pretty, former East German town of Salzwedel, a great culinary tradition has recently been revived and become immensely popular in Germany: it is a cake known as Baumkuchen, the 'tree cake'. It is fast becoming a popular special occasion

and wedding cake. It looks like a craggy tower of irregular rings draped in a satiny coat of white or dark chocolate icing. The intriguing shape prompts the question 'How do they do that?' The answer is that this cake is not baked in a tin, but built up with layers of batter which are spooned over a revolving hardwood roller in front of an open flame. It takes great skill to build up over 15 layers of mixture, so that when the cake is cut into wedges, it resembles the rings of a tree trunk.

Food for
Friends

Hands up those of you who love to party? Most of us, I suspect, along with millions of Germans too. With entertaining becoming more casual and relaxed, so food must be less fussy and easy to prepare. No other country understands this better than Germany where top quality sliced meats, sausages, pickles, cheeses and light rye breads can be turned almost effortlessly into fast and flash finger food. Needless to say, a good few German beers or some warming spiced Glühwein would match the mood and leave your guests with a party to remember. Even better, there won't be many pots and pans to wash up afterwards!

Above: a barbecue with fish, Bratwurst, courgette, tomatoes, skewers with Leberkäse and cherry tomatoes, Nuremberg grilling sausage, onion and Kasseler.

Sauerkraut and salami tray pizza
Sauerkraut- und Salami-Pizza vom Blech

Whether you've a large family feast to prepare or you're looking for a good savoury tray bake to serve cut in squares, there's a great selection of German foods for toppings. Use a base of a bread mix rolled to fit, then make a base of onion and Sauerkraut. For the topping choose a selection of sliced meats and grated cheeses. The following toppings are suggestions – you could vary them according to availability.

500 g pack bread mix – brown, mixed grain or light rye
1 onion, sliced thinly in rings
half 500 g jar Sauerkraut, drained and rinsed
100 g (3½ oz) herb, onion or cheese coated salami, sliced thinly
1 large tomato, sliced thinly
75 g (2¾ oz) Bavarian Emmental, coarsely grated
several good pinches of dried oregano or marjoram
freshly ground black pepper

1 Make up the bread mix according to pack instructions. Roll out on a lightly floured board to a thin rectangle large enough to fit a shallow roasting tin or baking tray, about 25 x 30 cm (10 x 12 inches). Lightly grease the tray with a little oil, but not too much or the bread will not press easily into it. Alternatively, line the tray base with a sheet of baking parchment. There is no need to let the dough prove.

2 Preheat the oven to Gas Mark 6/ 200°C/400°F. Scatter the onion rings and Sauerkraut evenly on top of the dough, making sure they reach right to the edges.

3 Now add your toppings – salami, sliced sausage, tomato and cheese. Sprinkle with herbs and black pepper.

4 Bake for 15–20 minutes until golden brown and bubbling. The bread base should be perfectly baked. Stand the pizza for 5 minutes before cutting into squares.

Mini onion tarts
Kleine Zwiebelfladen

In days gone by, leftover bread dough would be rolled into small rounds and topped with fried onion rings, Black Forest ham and soured cream then baked until bubbling and golden – it's Germany's answer to pizza!

Makes 6

500 g pack bread mix
2 large onions, sliced thinly
2 fat garlic cloves, crushed
40 g (1½ oz) lard or 3 tablespoons
    rapeseed oil
200 g (7 oz) Black Forest ham, roughly
    chopped
2 free-range egg yolks
4 tablespoons soured cream
a little freshly grated nutmeg
sea salt and freshly ground black pepper

1 Make up the bread dough according to pack instructions. Divide the dough into six balls and roll out to the size of a side plate on a lightly floured board. Place on two non-stick baking sheets and press down in the centre to form slight hollows. (This is so the egg yolk mix doesn't run off the topping.)

2 Prick the bases. Set aside to rise slightly while you make the toppings. Preheat the oven to Gas Mark 6/200°C/400°F.

3 Sauté the onions and garlic in the lard or oil for about 15 minutes until softened and golden brown. Remove with a slotted spoon and drain on paper towels, seasoning lightly.

4 Add the Black Forest ham to the pan and fry until slightly crisp. Don't over-crisp as it will be baked later.

5 Spread the onion between the six bread rounds and scatter over the ham. Beat the egg yolks with the soured cream and seasoning plus a little nutmeg.

6 Spoon over the six rounds, forking into the topping. Bake for 10 minutes then reduce the temperature to Gas Mark 4/180°C/350°F and bake for another 10 minutes until the dough is cooked. Remove onto a wire rack and cool. Serve warm.

6 slices wholemeal rye bread, sunflower
    seed bread or farm bread
2 fat garlic cloves, halved
about 2 tablespoons rapeseed oil
about 100 g (3½ oz) German soft cheese
    or cheese spread
2 ripe tomatoes, de-seeded and chopped
2 large leaves fresh basil, shredded thinly
about 100 g (3½ oz) sliced salami,
    Cervelat, garlic sausage, Bierwurst
    (optional)
sea salt and freshly ground black pepper

1 Preheat the oven to Gas Mark 6/200°C/ 400°F. Cut the bread slices in halves or quarters so they are the size of two good bites. Rub one side with the cut side of the garlic, then brush with the oil. Lay on a flat tray and bake for 10 minutes. Remove and cool.

2 When cold, spread with the soft cheese. Mix the tomato with the basil and seasoning and spoon on top of the cheese.

3 If using meats, slice into thin shreds and scatter on top. Serve immediately, sprinkled with more ground black pepper. Try crostini as an 'al fresco' starter.

Rye bread crostini

Roggenbrot-Crostini

Toast lightly oiled slices of rye bread in a hot oven and serve rubbed with garlic spread with soft German cheeses and topped with chopped tomato. Strips of salami or ham can be added as toppings for non-vegetarians. The bread bases can be made a few hours ahead.
Serves 6

Hot and crusty Frankfurter rolls
Frankfurter Würstchen im Schlafrock

Beer garden

These light crusty rolls appeal to all ages, from children and teenagers to adults of all decades! Simply roll crustless slices of white bread spread with mustard and ketchup (if used) around Frankfurters, then butter and bake for a few minutes until crisp. To add a tangy bite, add thin slivers of pickled cucumbers before rolling up. So easy to put together, even your children could make them. Ideally, choose bread slices that are slightly narrower than the Franks so they peek out attractively each side. Makes 6

6 large thin slices white bread
German sweet or medium-hot mustard,
     to spread
a little tomato ketchup (optional)
6 Frankfurters
1 pickled cucumber or about 3 gherkins,
     cut in long slivers (optional)
50 g (1¾ oz) butter, melted

1 Cut the crusts from the bread and, using a rolling pin, roll to make the bread a little pliable.

2 Spread thinly with the mustard making sure it reaches the edges evenly, then drizzle over a little ketchup, if used. Lay a Frankfurter at the top end and tuck in a couple or more of the cucumber or gherkin slivers (if used).

3 Roll up quite firmly, place join side down on a baking tray and secure with a wooden cocktail stick. Brush the top and sides with the melted butter.

4 Make 5 more rolls the same way then bake for 12–15 minutes until golden brown and crispy. Remove and cool until warm. Take out the sticks before serving.

Cold meat platter with radish and pickle salad

Garnierte Aufschnittplatte

The simplest serving ideas are invariably the most popular. German cold meats are the best quality and come in a glorious selection of shapes, colours and flavours. Calculating quantities when feeding a crowd can be a worry, but as leftovers can be wrapped and re-frigerated for another meal there's little fear of waste. Buy a little more than you will need, so you can arrange a tempting display. In general choose at least four varieties of sliced sausage, salami or ham allowing a total of 100 g (3½ oz) for each person. For example, choose a dark-coloured Cervelat or salami, a coated salami, Westphalian or Black Forest ham, a paler Bierwurst or Schinkenwurst and perhaps some cocktail-size Frankfurters or larger ones sliced on the diagonal.

In the centre arrange three small bowls of relishes, pickles or mustard-flavoured salads, such as this radish and pickled vegetable salad. Serve with a variety of German breads, pretzels or rolls.

Serves 4–6

a selection of sliced and cold meats of
    your choice – total weight about 500 g
    (1 lb)
1 bunch red radishes, trimmed and sliced
½ small green pepper, cored and chopped
Pickled carrot salad, drained
Pickled celeriac salad, drained
2 tablespoons sweet German mustard or
    mustard with herbs
3 tablespoons mayonnaise
2 tablespoons low-fat natural yogurt
2 tablespoons chopped fresh chives
    or 1 salad onion, chopped finely
sea salt and freshly ground black pepper

1 Mix the radishes, pepper, carrot and celeriac in a bowl. Season.

2 Beat the mustard, mayonnaise, yogurt and chives or onions, then stir into the vegetables.

3 Spoon into a bowl and place on the same tray or platter as the sliced meats.

Sausage and Sauerkraut filo turnovers

Würstchen & Sauerkraut-Taschen

Filo pastry is very similar to German Strudel pastry and can be used in the same ways. These savoury snacks can be prepared ahead and baked just before serving so they are warm and crisp.

Makes 12

4 large sheets of filo, about 25 x 30 cm (10 x 12 inches)
75 g (2¾ oz) butter, melted
2 Bratwurst or Bockwurst sausages, grilled and chopped
half 500 g jar Sauerkraut, drained and rinsed
75 g (2¾ oz) Bavarian smoked cheese, cut in small cubes

1 Cut the filo sheets lengthways into three. Keep them covered under a sheet of cling film as you work so they won't dry out.

2 Lay a strip along a board. Brush lightly with melted butter. Put a heaped teaspoon of Sauerkraut at one corner end. Press some chopped sausage on top, then 3–4 cheese cubes.

3 Fold over the filling wrapped in the filo on the diagonal, so it is completely enclosed in a triangle. Then flip over again, on the diagonal, and again and again until you get to the end of the filo strip and have a neat triangular turnover.

4 Place on a flat baking sheet. Repeat with the remaining ingredients until you have 12 turnovers. Brush the tops and sides with the remaining butter.

5 When ready to bake, preheat the oven to Gas Mark 6/200°C/400°F. Bake for 12–15 minutes until golden brown and crisp. Serve warm.

Schnaps

Schnaps means a 'gulp' in old German – and that is exactly how it should be drunk. There are two main types of Schnaps: Korn, a clear grain spirit, which is a good neutral liquor, similar to a vodka and ideal served as a beer chaser. Schnaps are always served on their own in small slender shot glasses, never with mixers. Secondly, there are the distilled spirits produced exclusively from fruit juices which ferment naturally without the addition of sugar or alcohol. Known collectively as Obstwasser, the most important is Kirschwasser made from late-ripening black cherries.

Party pastries with Quark
Gefüllte Quark Canapés

These party pastries can be made in advance and stored in an airtight container. Then an hour or two before your guests arrive, choose from the fillings below and decorate with a selection of garnishes. Don't fill the pastries too far in advance – the bases will become soft if you do.

If you don't have mini tartlet baking tins, simply cut out small pastry rounds and fit them into the normal size bun hole/jam tart tins. Don't worry if they don't fill each hole.

For a change from pastry cases, try using the fillings with Pumpernickel cocktail rounds or even crackers.

Pastry cases or boats
Makes 36 x 3-4 cm cases or small pastry boat shapes

300 g (10½ oz) plain flour
1 teaspoon sea salt
1 teaspoon dry mustard powder
150 g (5½ oz) cold unsalted butter
2 free-range egg yolks, beaten
a little ice cold water

1 Sift the flour, salt and mustard powder into a food processor or large mixing bowl. Cut the butter into small cubes and whizz or rub into the flour until the mixture resembles fine crumbs. Mix in the egg yolks and just enough water to make firm dough.

2 Turn the dough out onto a cold work surface and knead lightly until smooth. Wrap and chill

for 20 minutes. Heat the oven to Gas Mark 5/190°C/375°F.

3 Roll out on a lightly floured surface to the thickness of a £1 coin. If making pastry cases, cut out 5 cm (2-inch) rounds using a plain cutter. Re-roll once if necessary. Fit the rounds into three 12-hole bun tins (or bake 12 at a time and hold the rest covered in the fridge in between).

4 If making pastry boats, use pastry boat tins and lay the empty tins close together on a baking sheet. Lay the rolled-out dough on top. Press the dough gently into the cases, then roll the rolling pin on top so that the pastry will be cut by the edges of the tin. Prick the bases well with a fork.

5 Bake 'blind' for 10 minutes, pressing down any bubbles that may pop up. Cool slightly in the tins and then remove to cool on a wire tray. If making the boats in relays, cool the tin between each batch.

Fillings
Each recipe makes enough for 18 pastry cases.

Green Herb and Onion
200 g (7 oz) carton of Quark
2 salad onions, chopped finely
1 fat garlic clove, crushed
1 tablespoon chopped fresh parsley
1 tablespoon chopped fresh chives
1 tablespoon chopped fresh dill or chervil
2–3 tablespoons milk (optional)
sea salt and freshly ground black pepper

1 Beat the Quark in a bowl until smooth and creamy. Then mix in the onions, garlic, herbs and seasoning to taste. If you want a slightly softer mix, then add 2–3 tablespoons of milk. Chill until required.

Sweet Pepper and Paprika
1 small red pepper, cored and chopped finely
1 small yellow pepper, cored and chopped finely
1 fat garlic clove, crushed
2 tablespoons olive oil
1 teaspoon ground paprika
200 g (7 oz) carton of Quark
sea salt and freshly ground black pepper

1 Gently sauté the peppers and garlic in the oil in a saucepan for about 5–7 minutes until softened. Add the paprika during the last minute or so of cooking.

2 Cool completely, then add the mixture above including the pan juice to the Quark. Season well and chill until required.

Blue Cheese with Pear

100 g (3½ oz) Bavarian blue brie,
    rind removed
1 tablespoon celery, chopped
200 g carton of Quark
a little milk (optional)
2 small pears
a little fresh lemon juice
a few poppy seeds (optional)
sea salt and freshly ground black pepper

1 Mash the cheese with a fork in a bowl, then work in the celery and seasoning. Gradually beat in the Quark. If the mixture is a little stiff, mix in some milk for a nice dropping consistency. Chill until required.

2 Half an hour or so before serving, quarter, peel and core the pears, then cut crossways into slices. Mix with the lemon juice to stop them turning brown.

3 Fill the prepared pastry cases with the cheese mixture and stand a pear piece on top. Sprinkle lightly with poppy seeds to serve, if desired.

Curried Quark and Carrot

1 medium carrot, peeled and grated
    coarsely
200 g (7 oz) carton of Quark
2–3 tablespoons milk (optional)
1 teaspoon mild curry powder
2 teaspoons mango chutney
1 tablespoon chopped fresh coriander
sea salt and freshly ground black pepper

1 Mix the grated carrot with the Quark, milk (if using), curry, chutney, coriander and seasoning. Chill until required.

Prune and Katenspeck

4-5 no-need-to-cook prunes, soaked
50 g (1⅓ oz) Katenspeck, chopped finely
200 g (7 oz) carton of Quark
sea salt and freshly ground black pepper

1 Stone the prunes and then chop them finely. Heat a small frying pan and when hot, dry-fry the Katenspeck, stirring frequently over a medium high heat until crispy. Drain on kitchen paper and cool.

2 Mix the prunes and Katenspeck into the Quark and season to taste but be aware that it may not need much salt. Chill until required.

Quark Mini Quiches

Bake the filling and the pastry cases together, then cool and serve as bite-size quiches. This filling is enough for 18 mini quiches.

100 g (3¼ oz) Quark
3 tablespoons double cream
1 free-range egg, beaten
2 slices lean German cooked ham
    chopped finely
2 salad onions, chopped finely
sea salt and freshly ground black pepper

1 Line the bun tins with 18 uncooked pastry rounds and press well into the tins. Beat the Quark with the cream, egg and seasoning. Pour into a jug.

2 Heat the oven to Gas Mark 6/200°C/400°F. Mix together the chopped ham and onion, then divide between the pastry cases. Pour a little of the Quark liquid over each filled case. Make sure you don't overfill.

3 Bake for 10–12 minutes until the pastry is crisp and the filling risen. Cool for 5 minutes, then remove and cool completely. Serve at room temperature.

16 cloves
1 cinnamon stick
4–6 tablespoons sugar

1 Pour the wine into a large saucepan. Cut the lemon in quarters. Stick the cloves into the rind of one quarter. Slice the rest thinly.

2 Add the quarter and slices to the pan with the cinnamon and sugar.

3 Heat slowly until hot, but do not allow to boil. Serve in heatproof glasses or small cups. If you are worried about the glass breaking, stand a metal teaspoon in the glass before adding the hot liquid.

Spiced hot wine

Glühwein

At Christmas many German town centres have street markets with stalls selling biscuits, arty crafts, wooden toys and other festive nicknacks. Almost every street corner seems to boast Bratwurst and Glühwein stalls. It's amazing how revived one can feel after a small beaker of warm, spicy red wine. Below is a basic recipe, but in Germany, stalls will often offer you additional flavourings such as elderberry cordial or a shot of dark rum. Heat your Glühwein in a large saucepan on the stove or in a large jug in the microwave, but don't let it boil or all the alcohol will evaporate. If you want a less alcoholic drink, then mix in apple juice or water. But don't drink more as a result.

Serves 6

1 litre full-bodied red wine
1 small lemon

The Christchild's market in Nuremberg

Each year in virtually every town in Germany a Christkindlesmarkt is held, from the Friday before advent until Christmas Eve. The most famous is the one in Nuremberg.

The main purpose of the market is to sell Christmas tree decorations and traditional Christmas food, but before you assume that this is another typical 21st century consumerfest, the earliest record of the Nuremberg market dates from 1639. The story of the Christchild is celebrated with processions and Christmas plays and enactments of the nativity. Today visitors come from all over Europe and beyond to look at the beautifully decorated crib in the centre of the square and pause for reflection amidst the hectic pre-Christmas rush.

garnishes. It's all so brilliantly easy.

Here are some serving suggestions from Werner Seeberg, German Master Chef. Remember to keep them bite-sized so that each canapé can be popped into the mouth quickly. Garnishes should be subtle.

Cold canapés
From the top

- **Pumpernickel rounds with Matjes herring flakes, thinly sliced onion, cooked prawn, mayonnaise and dill garnish**
- **Toasted light rye bread with lettuce shreds, smoked salmon with horseradish cream and caviar or lump fish roe**
- **Country-style bread with Emmentaler cheese and chopped black grapes**
- **Pumpernickel rounds with Emmentaler cheese, cucumber, Quark, topped with chopped fresh herbs and thin red onion slices**
- **Cocktail pretzels with thinly sliced Bavarian blue brie**
- **Rounds of toast with folded and rolled slices of Black Forest ham, topped with green asparagus tips**
- **Cherry tomato shells filled with piped Quark and topped with finely chopped chives and tiny herb sprigs**

Party canapés
Party-Häppchen

If you like to make formal canapés, you'll find many German products ideal for shaping into dainty bite-sized finger food. Thinly sliced cold meats are easy to fold or roll; cheeses can be cut into neat squares or rounds; Vollkorn, rye and Pumpernickel breads can be stamped into shapes using small pastry cutters; Quark is ideal for flavouring and piping into swirls, while pickles and relishes are ideal as toppings and

Warm canapés

Prepare these ahead but don't heat until your guests are about to arrive. Otherwise, they will dry out if kept warm for too long.

From the top

- **Thin fresh apple slices (brushed with lemon juice), deep-fried Camembert wedges, topped with cranberry relish**
- **Country bread toast with honey-glazed Kassler with chopped fresh herbs**
- **Baby potato pancakes (or rosti) with hot pan-fried salmon fillet**
- **Toasted triangles baked with shredded Brunswick ham, pitted red grapes and grated Emmentaler cheese**

Christmas

Christmas in Germany, as nearly every-where else in the world today, is the biggest holiday and festival of the year. Celebrations traditionally begin on the first day of advent when carols are sung and the Christstollen, a cake with almonds, marzipan, orange and lemon juice, rosewater and raisins, is cut. Most German homes have an advent wreath with four thick red candles. Each Sunday in advent a candle is lit.

On the 6th December an earlier incarnation of Father Christmas, St Nicholas, fills a boot with sweets, apples or nuts for good children. Bad children get nothing at all, or a stick for their parents to punish them with!

A pine or fir tree is decorated on Christmas Eve and Father Christmas brings the presents to the eager children.

PILS Universally popular, Pils is a good all-round lager-style, bottom-fermented light beer made in many regions of Germany. It has a strong, hoppy aroma and flavour, with what experts describe as a long dry finish. Bavarian Pils has a more malty taste. Both average 4.8-5% alcohol.

Germany's number one drink for over 1000 years

Beer

Given beer's popularity in Germany, it is probably not surprising there are now well over 5000 varieties brewed in 1500 breweries. A good fifth of these are found in the southern region of Bavaria, the capital of which is Munich, home to the world-famous October beer festival. Many styles and strengths have developed over the years. Beer is drunk at different times during the day, generally with meals or alongside the most popular bar nibble, lightly salted pretzels.

So seriously was the science of brewing taken in the past that it gave rise to what was perhaps Europe's first food purity law, passed in 1516 by Duke William IV of Bavaria, and still in force today. The law stated that only barley, malt, hops and water were allowed in the beer-making process – a revolutionary edict in the days when adulteration of foodstuffs was rife.

ALTBIER AND KÖLSCH
These are aromatic, hoppy, bitter beers. Altbier is darker; it is similar in style to UK ales. Kölsch is lighter. They are good beers for everyday drinking.

EXPORT, PILS AND DARK BEER Dark beer
(Schwarzbier) is aromatic and malty. Export
beers vary depending on the region but in
general they are full-bodied, malty, light to
dark brews.

BERLINER WEISSE WITH RASPBERRY
AND BERLINER WEISSE WITH WOODRUFF
CORDIAL When Berliners want a good
thirst-quencher, they order a Berliner Weisse
– a Berlin wheat beer. Lightly fizzy and pale,
with a flavour described as milky-sour, these
beers are often flavoured with a shot of
raspberry or herb woodruff cordial.

WHEAT BEERS: KRISTALL, HEFE AND
DARK Described as having the zest of a
lager and the complexity of an ale with a
bubblegum finish, these are totally distinct,
lightly spicy wheat and barley malt beers
brewed in a variety of strengths.

BOCKBIER These are 'big' flavour beers
with a malty, aromatic and lightly hoppy
bitterness and ideal for those who like a
strong brew. Colours range from light golden
to dark.

Shopping guide

There is a huge variety of German food and drink available in supermarkets, food halls and delicatessens. In supermarkets you'll often find that German products are sold under the supermarket's own label. Most of the products mentioned in this book are widely available and you should have no problem in finding them in the shops.

Authenticity

At Christmas you'll find many different versions of Stollen in the shops, but for a true taste of Germany you need to make sure that yours was produced in Germany. Generally, you should have a look at the labels of German food and drink products. In most cases, if they're the genuine article there will be an oval-shaped 'healthmark' on the label with a 'D' indicating Germany. Beware of 'German-style' products – they are generally not the real thing.

Meat and sausages

Supermarkets, food halls and delicatessens stock a wide range of sliced sausages, such as pepper salami, Westphalian ham and unsliced sausages such as meat sausage. The self-service chiller cabinet sells pre-packed and pre-sliced sausages. Frankfurters are most commonly available packed in jars, though you'll also see them in tins and larger vacuum packs. Bratwurst is available in vacuum packs as are Nuremberg grilling sausages.

Cheese and dairy products

You'll find German cheeses and other dairy items both prepacked in chiller cabinets and at the deli counter of your local supermarket. The chameleon of German cheeses, Quark, is usually found next to cottage cheese. Look for German yogurts and Quark desserts in the usual yogurt and chilled dessert section.

Beers

Lots of beers have German-sounding names, so do read the label to make sure that a beer is brewed according to Germany's purity law (see page 124). With over 1200 breweries in Germany, there is no instantly recognisable national German brand – although you probably know one or two already.

Breads

Surprisingly there is a good variety of freshly baked German bread available in the UK. Supermarkets and other stores import frozen sourdough and rye bread dough and bake the breads on site. You'll also find pre-sliced German breads in supermarket bakery sections and occasionally in the crispbread sections.

Biscuits, cakes and confectionery

Black Forest cake and Apfelstrudel can be found in the frozen foods section. The best time to find German biscuits and confectionery in the shops is at Christmas. Look out for Christmas biscuits, Lebkuchen and genuine German Stollen from the end of October throughout the festive season in supermarkets, food halls and delicatessen shops.

White asparagus

This is quite an elusive delicacy but it's not impossible to find in the large London food halls. The season is short though – it only lasts for six weeks at the most from May until mid June. Perhaps freeze some so that you can enjoy it at any time of year.

If you have any questions regarding food and drink from Germany please write to: CMA UK, 17a Church Road, Wimbledon, London SW19 5DQ

Index